Desire

To solve our human problems and enable us to find everlasting peace and happiness, Buddha gave the most profound teachings for us to use as practical advice. His teachings are known as "Dharma," which means supreme protection from suffering. Dharma is the actual method to solve our human problems. To understand this, we should first consider what is the real nature of our problems and what are their main causes.

Our problems do not exist outside our mind. The real nature of our problems is our unpleasant feelings, which are part of our mind. When our car, for example, has a problem we often say, "I have a problem," but in reality it is not our problem but the car's problem. Our problems develop only when we experience unpleasant feelings. The car's problems exist outside the mind, whereas our problems are inside our mind. By differentiating between animate and inanimate problems like this, we can understand that the real nature of our problems is our own feelings, which are part of our mind.

All our problems—our unpleasant feelings—come from our delusions of attachment and self-grasping ignorance, therefore these delusions are the main causes of our problems. We have strong attachment to the fulfillment of our own wishes and for this aim we work very hard throughout our life, experiencing many difficulties and problems. When our wishes are not fulfilled we experience unhappiness and depression, which often causes us to become angry, creating more problems for both ourself and others. We can understand this clearly through our own experience. When we lose our friends, job, status, or reputation and so forth, we experience pain and many difficulties. This is because of our strong attachment to these things. If we did not have such attachment, there would be no basis for experiencing suffering and problems at their loss.

Due to strong attachment to our own views, we immediately experience the inner problem of unpleasant feelings when someone opposes them. This causes us to become angry, which leads to arguments and conflicts with others, and this in turn gives rise to further problems. Most political problems experienced throughout the world are caused by people with strong attachment to their own views. Many problems are also caused by people's attachment to their religious views.

In previous lives, because of our attachment to fulfilling our own wishes, we performed many different actions that harmed other living beings. As a result of these actions, we now experience many different problems and sufferings in our life.

If we look in the mirror of Dharma, we can see

how our attachment, anger and especially our self-grasping ignorance are the causes of all our problems and sufferings. We will definitely realize that unless we control these delusions there is no other method to solve our human problems. Dharma is the only method to control our delusions of attachment, anger and self-grasping ignorance. This is why we can say that Buddha's teachings, Dharma, are the only method to solve our human problems. Ancient Kadampa practitioners and many practitioners of today understand this through their own experience—they are witnesses to this truth. Buddha's teachings are the supreme scientific method to solve human problems. If we sincerely put his teachings into practice, we will definitely solve our human problems and find the real meaning of our life.

Maintain harmony and joy all the time

Suffering

In *Sutra of the Four Noble Truths*, Buddha says:

> You should know sufferings.
> You should abandon origins.
> You should attain cessations.
> You should practice the path.

These instructions are known as the "four noble truths." They are called "noble truths" because they are superior and non-deceptive instructions.

In general, everyone who has physical or mental pain, even animals, understands their own suffering. But when Buddha says, "You should know sufferings," he means that we should know the sufferings of our future lives. Through knowing these we will develop a strong wish to liberate ourself from them. This practical advice is important for everybody, because if we have the wish to liberate ourself from the sufferings of future lives, we will definitely use our present human life for the freedom and happiness of our countless future lives. There is no greater meaning than this.

If we do not have this wish, we will waste our precious

human life only for the freedom and happiness of this one short life. This would be foolish because our intention and actions would be no different from the intention and actions of animals who are only concerned with this life alone. The Great Yogi Milarepa once said to a hunter called Gonpo Dorje:

Your body is human but your mind is that of an animal.
You, a human being, who possess an animal's mind, please listen to my song.

Normally we believe that solving the problems and sufferings of our present life is most important, and we dedicate our whole life for this purpose. In reality, the duration of the problems and sufferings of this life is very short; if we die tomorrow, they will end tomorrow. However, since the duration of the problems and sufferings of future lives is endless, the freedom and happiness of our future lives is vastly more important than the freedom and happiness of this one short life. With the first noble truth, Buddha encourages us to use our present human life to prepare for the freedom and happiness of our countless future lives. Those who do this are truly wise.

A detailed explanation to help us understand future lives can be found in Appendices I and II.

Origins

"You should abandon origins."

This is also very practical advice. "Origins" refers mainly to our delusions of attachment, anger and self-grasping ignorance. Normally we have a sincere wish to avoid suffering permanently, but we never think to abandon our delusions. However, without controlling and abandoning our delusions, it is impossible to attain permanent liberation from suffering and problems. Therefore, we should follow Buddha's advice, and through our concentration on the profound meaning of Dharma and the force of our determination, emphasize controlling our attachment, anger and other delusions.

Delusions are called "origins" because they are the source of all sufferings and the main cause of all our problems. We have already seen how attachment is one of the main causes of our problems, and the problems caused by anger will be explained in Part Two. The following brief explanation will show how our self-grasping is the principal cause of all our problems.

First we should recognize our self-grasping, which always abides at our heart destroying our inner peace.

Its nature is a wrong awareness that mistakenly believes ourself and others to be truly, or inherently, existent. This is an ignorant mind because in reality things do not exist inherently—they exist as mere imputations. Because the foolish mind of self-grasping believes or grasps at "I," "mine" and all other phenomena as truly existent, we develop attachment to those things we like and hatred for those we do not like. We then perform various actions that harm other living beings and, as a result, we experience various sufferings and problems throughout this life and in life after life; this is the fundamental reason why we experience so many problems. Because our sense of truly existent "I" and "mine" is so strong, our self-grasping also acts as the basis of all our daily problems.

Self-grasping can be likened to a poisonous tree, other delusions to its branches and all our sufferings to its fruits. It is the fundamental source of all other delusions and all our sufferings and problems. Understanding this, we should apply great effort to recognize, reduce and finally abandon this ignorance completely.

Cessations

"You should attain cessations."

This means that we should attain the permanent cessation of suffering. Generally, from time to time, everybody experiences a temporary cessation of particular sufferings. For instance, those who are physically healthy are experiencing a temporary cessation of sickness. However, this is not enough because it is only temporary. Later, they will have to experience the suffering of sickness again and again, in this life and in countless future lives. Every living being without exception has to experience the cycle of the sufferings of sickness, aging, death and rebirth, in life after life, endlessly. Following Buddha's example, we should develop strong renunciation for this endless cycle. When he was living in the palace with his family, Buddha saw how his people were constantly experiencing these sufferings and he made the strong determination to attain enlightenment, the permanent cessation of suffering, and to lead every living being to this state.

Buddha did not encourage us to abandon daily activities that provide necessary conditions for living, or that prevent poverty, environmental problems, particular diseases and so forth. However, no matter how successful we are in these activities, we will never achieve permanent cessation of such problems. We will still have to experience them in our countless future lives, and even in this life, although we work very hard to prevent these problems, the sufferings of poverty, environmental pollution and disease are increasing throughout the world. Furthermore, because of the power of modern technology, there are now many great dangers developing in the world that have never been experienced before. Therefore, we should not be satisfied with just temporary freedom from particular sufferings, but apply great effort to attain permanent freedom while we have this opportunity.

We should consider the preciousness of our human life. Because of their previous deluded views that denied the value of spiritual practice, those who have taken rebirth as animals, for example, have no opportunity to engage in spiritual practice that alone gives rise to a meaningful life. Since it is impossible for them to listen to, understand, contemplate and meditate on spiritual instructions, their present animal rebirth itself is an obstacle. Only human beings are free from such obstacles and have all the necessary conditions for engaging in spiritual paths, which alone lead to everlasting peace and happiness. This combination of freedom and possession of necessary conditions is the special characteristic that makes our human life so precious.

The Path

"You should practice the path."

In this context, "path" does not mean an external path that leads from one place to another, but an inner path, a spiritual path that leads us to the pure happiness of liberation and enlightenment. A detailed explanation of the stages of the path to liberation and enlightenment can be found in *Modern Buddhism, Transform Your Life, The New Meditation Handbook* and *Joyful Path of Good Fortune*.

The practice of the stages of the path to liberation can be condensed within the three trainings of higher moral discipline, higher concentration and higher wisdom. These trainings are called "higher" because they are motivated by renunciation, a sincere wish to attain permanent liberation from the sufferings of this life and future lives. They are therefore the actual path to liberation that we need to practice.

The nature of moral discipline is abandoning inappropriate actions, maintaining pure behavior and performing every action correctly with a virtuous motivation. Moral discipline is most important for everybody in order to prevent future problems for oneself and for others. It makes us pure because it makes our actions pure. We need to be clean and pure ourself; just having a clean body is not enough, since our body is not our self. Moral discipline is like a great earth that supports and nurtures the crops of spiritual realizations. Without practicing moral discipline, it is very difficult to make progress in spiritual trainings. Training in higher moral discipline is learning to be deeply familiar with the practice of moral discipline, motivated by renunciation.

The second higher training is training in higher concentration. The nature of concentration is preventing distractions and concentrating on virtuous objects. It is very important to train in concentration, because with distractions we cannot accomplish anything. Training in higher concentration is learning to be deeply familiar with the ability to stop distractions and concentrate on virtuous objects, motivated by renunciation. With regard to any Dharma practice, if our concentration is clear and strong it is very easy to make progress. Normally our main problem is distractions. The practice of moral discipline prevents gross distractions, and concentration prevents subtle distractions; together they give rise to quick results in our Dharma practice.

The third higher training is training in higher wisdom. The nature of wisdom is a virtuous intelligent mind whose functions are to dispel confusion and to understand profound objects thoroughly. Many people are very intelligent in destroying their enemies, caring for their families, finding what they want and so forth, but this is not wisdom. Even animals have such intelligence. Worldly intelligence is deceptive, whereas wisdom will never deceive us. It is our inner Spiritual Guide who leads us to correct paths, and is the divine eye through which we can see past and future lives and the special connection between our actions and our experiences, known as "karma." The subject of karma is very extensive and subtle, and we can understand it only through wisdom. Training in higher wisdom is meditating on wisdom realizing emptiness, motivated by renunciation. This wisdom is extremely profound. Its object, emptiness, is not nothingness but is the real nature of all phenomena. A detailed explanation of emptiness can be found in *Transform Your Life* and *Modern Buddhism*.

Worldly intelligence is deceptive, whereas wisdom will never deceive us.

The three higher trainings are the actual method to attain the permanent cessation of the sufferings of this life and of countless future lives. This can be understood by the following analogy. When we cut a tree using a saw, the saw alone cannot cut the tree without the use of our hands, which in turn depend upon our body. Training in higher moral discipline is like our body, training in higher concentration is like our hands and training in higher wisdom is like the saw. By using these three together, we can cut the poisonous tree of our self-grasping ignorance, and automatically all other delusions—its branches—and all our sufferings and problems—its fruits—will cease completely. Then we will have attained the permanent cessation of suffering in this life and future lives—the supreme permanent inner peace known as "nirvana," or liberation. We will have solved all our human problems and accomplished the real meaning of our life.

The four noble truths can be understood and practiced on many different levels. Directly or indirectly, all Dharma practices are included within the practice of the four noble truths. Through the above instructions we can understand in general how to practice them. We should also understand how to practice them with regard to particular sufferings, origins, cessations and paths; for example, the suffering of anger, its origin (which is anger itself), its cessation (the true cessation of the suffering of anger) and the path that is the practice of patience. This will be explained in Part Two.

PART TWO

Patience

Take the precious jewels of wisdom and compassion from the treasure vase of Kadam Dharma

Patience

The following explanation of how to overcome our anger through practicing patience is based on *Guide to the Bodhisattva's Way of Life*, the famous poem by the great Buddhist Master Shantideva. Although composed over a thousand years ago, this is one of the clearest and most powerful explanations of the subject ever written, and is just as relevant today as it was then.

Shantideva says:

There is no evil greater than anger,
And no virtue greater than patience.
Therefore, I should strive in various ways
To become familiar with the practice of patience.

Enjoy the purity of your mind and actions

The Faults of Anger

Anger is one of the most common and destructive delusions, and it afflicts our mind almost every day. To solve the problem of anger, we first need to recognize the anger within our mind, acknowledge how it harms both ourself and others and appreciate the benefits of being patient in the face of difficulties. We then need to apply practical methods in our daily life to reduce our anger and finally to prevent it from arising at all.

What is anger? Anger is a deluded mind that focuses on an animate or inanimate object, feels it to be unattractive, exaggerates its bad qualities and wishes to harm it. For example, when we are angry with our partner, at that moment he or she appears to us as unattractive or unpleasant. We then exaggerate his bad qualities by focusing only on those aspects that irritate us and ignoring all his good qualities and kindness, until we have built up a mental image of an intrinsically faulty person. We then wish to harm him in some way, probably by criticizing or disparaging him. Because it is based on an exaggeration, anger is an unrealistic mind; the intrinsically faulty person or thing that it focuses on does not in fact exist. Moreover, as we will see, anger is also an extremely destructive mind that serves no useful purpose whatsoever. Having understood the nature and disadvantages of anger, we then need to watch our mind carefully at all times in order to recognize it whenever it begins to arise.

There is nothing more destructive than anger. It destroys our peace and happiness in this life and impels us to engage in negative actions that lead to untold suffering in future lives. It blocks our spiritual progress and prevents us from accomplishing any spiritual goals we have set for ourself—from merely improving our mind, up to full enlightenment. The opponent to anger is patient acceptance, and if we are seriously interested in progressing along the spiritual path, there is no practice more important than this.

In *Guide to the Bodhisattva's Way of Life*, Shantideva says that all the merit, or good fortune, created in our mind through the virtuous actions we have performed over thousands of eons can be destroyed in an instant by getting angry with a holy being such as a Bodhisattva. A Bodhisattva is someone who has bodhichitta, the spontaneous wish to attain enlightenment for the benefit of all living beings. Since bodhichitta is an internal quality, it is not easy to tell who is and who is not a Bodhisattva. It is very possible that a famous Spiritual Teacher is not a Bodhisattva whereas someone living simply and quietly among a group of needy people is, in fact, such a highly realized being. If as Shantideva says, a moment of anger toward someone who has developed bodhichitta can destroy eons of virtue, it is therefore advisable not to generate anger toward anyone.

Anger can arise toward many different objects, and if it is directed toward someone who has high spiritual realizations it can destroy the merit we have accumulated over thousands of lifetimes. Similarly, if we generate intense anger toward those from whom we have received great kindness, whether materially

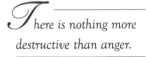

There is nothing more destructive than anger.

or spiritually, there will be no limit to the destruction of our merit or good fortune. Even anger directed toward someone who is our equal can destroy the good fortune collected over many previous lifetimes.

Suppose that one day we create a vast amount of merit by making extensive offerings to the Three Jewels—Buddha, Dharma and Sangha—or by helping many people. If we remember to dedicate our merit to the attainment of enlightenment and the benefit of all sentient beings, this merit is safe and cannot be destroyed by anger. However, if this merit is not properly dedicated, and on the following day we get very angry with someone, the virtue accumulated from the previous day's practice will become powerless. Even if we only get slightly angry, this can delay the ripening of our virtuous karma. Thus, the delusion of anger harms us severely. An alcoholic drink has the potential to intoxicate us, but if it is boiled this potential is destroyed. In the same way, the practice of virtue creates in our mind the potential for us to experience happiness, but anger can destroy this potential completely.

The destruction of merit is one of the invisible faults of anger and therefore something that we can only accept on faith. There are, however, many visible faults of this delusion, and the need to develop patience will become obvious once we look at these more manifest shortcomings.

Anger is by nature a painful state of mind. Whenever we develop anger, our inner peace immediately disappears and even our body becomes tense and uncomfortable. We are so restless that we find it nearly impossible to fall asleep, and whatever sleep we do manage to get is fitful and unrefreshing. It is impossible to enjoy ourself when we are angry, and even the food we eat seems unpalatable. Anger transforms even a normally attractive person into an ugly red-faced demon. We grow more and more miserable, and no matter how hard we try we cannot control our emotions.

One of the most harmful effects of anger is that it robs us of our reason and good sense. Wishing to retaliate against those whom we think have harmed us, we expose ourself to great personal danger merely to exact petty revenge. To get even for perceived injustices or slights, we are prepared to jeopardize our job, our relationships and even the well-being of our family and children. When we are angry we lose all freedom of choice, driven here and there by an uncontrollable rage. Sometimes this blind rage is even directed at our loved ones and benefactors. In a fit of anger, forgetting the immeasurable kindness we have received from our friends, family or Spiritual

Teachers, we might strike out against and even kill the ones we hold the most dear. It is no wonder that a habitually angry person is soon avoided by all who know him. This unfortunate victim of his own temper is the despair of those who formerly loved him, and eventually finds himself abandoned by everyone.

Anger is particularly destructive in relationships. When we live in close contact with someone, our personalities, priorities, interests and ways of doing things frequently clash. Since we spend so much time together, and since we know the other person's shortcomings so well, it is very easy for us to become critical and short-tempered with our partner and to blame him or her for making our life uncomfortable. Unless we make a continuous effort to deal with this anger as it arises, our relationship will suffer. A couple may genuinely love one another, but, if they frequently get angry with each other, the times when they are happy together will become fewer and further between. Eventually, there will come a point when before they have recovered from one argument the next has already begun. Like a flower choked by weeds, love cannot survive in such circumstances.

In a close relationship, opportunities to get angry arise many times a day, so to prevent the build-up of bad feelings we need to deal with anger as soon as it begins to arise in our mind. We clear away the dishes after every meal rather than waiting until the end of the month, because we do not want to live in a dirty house nor be faced with a huge, unpleasant job. In the same way, we need to make the effort to clear away the mess in our mind as soon as it appears, because if we allow it to accumulate it will become more and more difficult to deal with, and will endanger our relationship. We should remember that every opportunity to develop anger is also an opportunity to develop patience. A relationship in which there is a lot of friction and conflict of interest is also an unrivalled opportunity to erode away our self-cherishing and self-grasping, which are the real sources of all our problems. By practicing the instructions on patience explained in this book, we can transform our relationships into opportunities for spiritual growth.

If we really want to be rid of all enemies, all we need to do is uproot our own anger.

It is through our anger and hatred that we transform people into enemies. We generally assume that anger arises when we encounter a disagreeable person, but actually it is the anger already within us that transforms the person we meet into our imagined foe. Someone controlled by anger lives within a paranoid view of the world, surrounded by enemies of his or her own creation. The false belief that everyone hates him can become so overwhelming that he might even go insane, the victim of his own delusion.

It often happens that in a group there is one person who always blames the others for what goes wrong. Yet it is generally the person who complains who is responsible for whatever disharmony arises. The story is told of an old woman who used to argue and fight with everyone. She was so disagreeable that eventually she was expelled from her village. When she arrived at another village the people there asked her, "Why did you leave your home?" She replied, "Oh, all the people in that village were wicked; I left in order to escape from them." The people thought it odd that a whole village could be so bad and concluded that it was the old lady herself who was at fault. Fearing that she would cause them nothing but trouble, they threw her out of their village as well.

It is very important to identify the actual cause of whatever unhappiness we feel. If we are forever blaming our difficulties on others, this is a clear sign that there are still many problems and faults within our own mind. If we were truly peaceful inside and had our mind under control, difficult people or circumstances would not be able to disturb this peace, and so we would feel no compulsion to blame anyone or regard them as our enemy. To someone who has subdued his or her mind and eradicated the last trace of anger, all beings are friends. A Bodhisattva, for instance, whose sole motivation is to benefit others, has no enemies. Very few people wish to harm someone who is a friend of all the world, and even if someone did harm him or her, the Bodhisattva would not view this person as an enemy. With his mind dwelling in patience, he would remain calm and untroubled, and his love and respect for his assailant would be undiminished. Such is the power of a well-controlled mind. Therefore, if we really want to be rid of all enemies, all we need to do is uproot our own anger.

We should not think that this is an impossible goal. By

relying on the appropriate methods, many people have been able to cure themselves completely of their physical illnesses. In the same way, it is certainly possible to eradicate the inner disease of anger, and many spiritual practitioners of the past have succeeded in doing so. Methods to gain release from this crippling delusion exist and have proven their effectiveness whenever people have sincerely put them into practice, and there is no reason why they cannot work for us as well. Imagine what the world would be like if we all conquered our anger! The danger of war would evaporate, armies would become unnecessary and soldiers would have to look elsewhere for work. Machine guns, tanks and nuclear weapons—instruments useful only to the angry mind—could be put away, as all conflicts, from wars between nations to arguments between individuals, came to an end. Even if this universal peace and harmony seems too much to hope for, imagine the freedom and peace of mind each of us individually would enjoy if we managed to free ourself completely from the distorted and destructive mind of anger.

Having understood the many faults of anger, we should watch our mind closely at all times. As soon as we notice our mind starting to get agitated—for example when dwelling on someone's faults and blaming him or her for the unpleasant feelings in our mind—we should immediately recall the faults of anger. Remembering that getting angry will solve nothing and only create more suffering for both ourself and others, we should then make the effort to channel our mind in a more constructive direction.

If we are able to recognize a negative train of thought before it develops into full-blown anger, it is not too hard to control. If we can do this, there is no danger of our anger being "bottled up" and turning into resentment. Controlling anger and repressing anger are two very different things. Repression occurs when anger has developed fully in our mind but we fail to acknowledge its presence. We pretend to ourself and to others that we are not angry—we control the outward expression of anger but not the anger itself. This is very dangerous because the anger continues to seethe below the surface of our mind, gathering in strength until one day it inevitably explodes.

On the other hand, when we control anger we see exactly what is going on in our mind. We acknowledge honestly the angry stirrings in our mind for what they are, realize that allowing them to grow will only result in suffering, and then make a free and conscious decision to respond more constructively. If we do this skillfully, anger does not get a chance to develop properly, and so there is nothing to repress. Once we learn to control and overcome our anger in this way, we will always find happiness, both in this life and in our future lives. Those who truly wish to be happy, therefore, should make the effort to free their minds from the poison of anger.

To summarize, for as long as our mind is filled with anger we will not find happiness either in this life or in lives to come. Anger is our real enemy, and until we evict it from our mind it will continue to cause us unimaginable suffering. Therefore, instead of blaming other people or circumstances and viewing these as our enemies, we should recognize that it is the anger within our mind that is the real source of our suffering. Then, through guarding our mind with continuous mindfulness and alertness, we should take every opportunity to free our mind from its destructive influence.

Why We Get Angry

To reduce and finally eradicate our anger we need to tackle the problem from two sides. Firstly, we need to gain a clear recognition of the many faults of anger as already explained—identifying this poisonous delusion, and not any external force, as our true enemy. This recognition awakens within us an urgent desire to rid ourself of anger as soon as possible. If we discovered that we had inadvertently swallowed poison, we would naturally develop an urgent wish to get rid of it because we understand the harm that it will cause. Yet the inner poison of anger harms us far more than any physical poison—its venom reaching even into our future lives— so our desire to eliminate it should be that much stronger!

Secondly, we need to gain a deep understanding of why we become angry and then work to counteract and eliminate the causes we have uncovered. The root cause of anger, as of all other delusions, is our innate self-grasping ignorance—the mistaken view that holds ourself and all other phenomena to be inherently existent. Once we have cut through this ignorance, there will no longer be any basis in our mind for unhappiness, dissatisfaction or any delusions. Self-grasping is a deeply entrenched habit of mind. To eradicate it completely, we need to develop a direct realization of emptiness, which is not something we can do overnight. There are, however, other more immediate causes of anger, and since these can be dealt with right away, it is worthwhile concentrating on them during the early stages of our practice.

Anger is a response to feelings of unhappiness, which in turn arise whenever we meet with unpleasant circumstances. Whenever we are prevented from fulfilling our wishes, or forced into a situation we dislike—in short, whenever we have to put up with something we would rather avoid—our uncontrolled mind reacts by immediately feeling unhappy. This uncomfortable feeling can easily turn into anger, and we become even more disturbed than before.

It is a very useful exercise to examine the kinds of situation in which we get angry. We will probably find that most of our anger arises when our desires are frustrated and we do not get what we want. For example, a man who very much wants to be with his lover will be extremely resentful of anyone or anything that prevents him from doing this. If his lover refuses to see him, or leaves him for someone else, his unhappiness can easily turn into rage. It is essential that we learn new ways of relating to frustrations and disappointments. Since it is unreasonable to expect that we can fulfill all our wants and desires, we must cultivate a more realistic and balanced approach to them.

The other main reason we become unhappy and angry is because we are faced with a situation we do not want or like. Every day we encounter hundreds of situations we do not like, from stubbing our toe or having a disagreement with our partner, to discovering that our house has burned down or that we have cancer; and our normal reaction to all of these occurrences is to become unhappy and angry. However, try as we might we cannot prevent unpleasant things from happening to us. We cannot promise that for the rest of the day nothing bad will happen to us; we cannot even promise that we will be alive to see the end of the day. In samsara we are not in control of what happens to us.

We need to find a different way of relating to frustrated desires and unwanted occurrences.

Since it is impossible to fulfill all our desires or to stop unwanted things from happening to us, we need to find a different way of relating to frustrated desires and unwanted occurrences. We need to learn patient acceptance.

Patience is a mind that is able to accept, fully and happily, whatever occurs. It is much more than just gritting our teeth and putting up with things. Being patient means to welcome wholeheartedly whatever arises, having given up the idea that things should be other than what they are. It is always possible to be patient; there is no situation so bad that it cannot be accepted patiently, with an open, accommodating and peaceful heart.

When patience is present in our mind it is impossible for unhappy thoughts to gain a foothold. There are many examples of people who have managed to practice patience even in the most extreme circumstances, such as under torture or in the final ravages of cancer. Although their body was ruined beyond repair, deep down their mind remained at peace. By learning to accept the small difficulties and hardships that arise every day in the course of our lives, gradually our capacity for patient acceptance will increase and we will come to know for ourself the freedom and joy that true patience brings.

If we practice the patience of voluntarily accepting suffering, we can maintain a peaceful mind even when experiencing suffering and pain. If we maintain this peaceful and positive state of mind through the force of mindfulness, unhappy minds will have no opportunity to arise. On the other hand, if we allow ourself to dwell on unhappy thoughts there will be no way for us to prevent anger from arising. For this reason Geshe Chekhawa said, "Always rely upon a happy mind alone."

As mentioned above, the main reason we become unhappy is because our wishes are not fulfilled or we have to deal with an unpleasant situation. However, as Shantideva says in *Guide to the Bodhisattva's Way of Life*:

> If something can be remedied
> Why be unhappy about it?
> And if there is no remedy for it,
> There is still no point in being unhappy.

If there is a way to remedy an unpleasant, difficult situation, what point is there in being unhappy? On the other hand, if it is completely impossible to remedy the situation or to fulfill our wishes, there is also no reason to get upset, because how will becoming unhappy help? This line of reasoning is very useful because we can apply it to any situation.

Patient acceptance does not necessarily mean that we do not take practical steps to improve our situation. If it is possible to remedy the situation, then of course we should; but to do this we do not need to become unhappy and impatient. For example, when we have a headache, there is no contradiction between practicing patience and taking medicine, but until the medicine takes effect we need to accept whatever discomfort we feel with a calm and patient mind. If instead of accepting our present pain we become unhappy and fight against it, we will just become tense, and as a result it will take longer to get rid of our headache. For as long as we are in samsara, we cannot avoid unpleasant, difficult situations and a certain amount of physical discomfort, but by training our mind to look at frustrating situations in a more realistic manner, we can free ourself from a lot of unnecessary mental suffering.

There are innumerable occasions when it is easy to develop an unhappy mind. When we ourself, our family or our friends are mistreated, blamed or are experiencing any kind of misfortune, we normally react by becoming unhappy. We also become unhappy when our relationships are difficult, when we have financial or health problems, when we lose what is dear to us, when we are lonely or can never find the time to be alone, when we cannot find work or have too much work, when our dreams and wishes remain unfulfilled or, once fulfilled, leave us feeling hollow and dissatisfied, when we fail or when our success brings with it more stress than we can bear or when people we dislike are successful—the list is endless. In all these situations our unhappiness can easily lead to a feeling that life or other people are unfair to us, and this depresses us even more.

When we stop seeing other people as problems they stop being problems.

Instead of reacting blindly through the force of emotional habit, we should examine whether it is helpful or realistic to become unhappy in such situations. We do not need to become unhappy just because things do not go our way. Although until now this has indeed been our reaction to difficulties, but once we recognize that it does not work we are free to respond in a more realistic and constructive way.

Patient acceptance is often thought to be a weak and passive response to problems that we have neither the power nor the courage to solve. In reality, however, being patient is far from being passive. There is nothing strong or courageous in reacting to hardship or insults with anger—all we are doing is being defeated by our delusions. On the other hand, by standing up to our delusions and refusing to fall into our well-worn mental grooves of intolerance and non-acceptance, we are taking a very strong, active stance.

In reality, most of our emotional problems are nothing more than a failure to accept things as they are—in which case it is patient acceptance, rather than attempting to change externals, that is the solution. For example, many of our relationship problems arise because we do not accept our partner as he or she is. In these cases the solution is not to change our partner into what we would like him to be, but to accept him fully as he is. There are many levels of acceptance. Perhaps we already try to tolerate our partner's idiosyncrasies, refrain from criticizing him or her and go along with his wishes most of the time; but in the depths of our heart have we given up judging him? Are we completely free from resentment and blaming? Is there not still a subtle thought that he should be different from the way he is? True patience involves letting go of all these thoughts.

Once we fully accept other people as they are without the slightest judgment or reservation—the way all enlightened beings accept us—then there is no basis for problems in our relations with others. Problems do not exist outside our mind, so when we stop seeing other people as problems they stop being problems. The person who is a problem to a non-accepting mind does not exist in the calm, clear space of patient acceptance.

Patient acceptance not only helps us, it also helps those with whom we are patient. Being accepted feels very different from being judged. When someone feels judged, they automatically become tight and defensive, but when they feel accepted they can relax, and this allows their good qualities to come to the surface. Patience always solves our inner problems, but often it solves problems between people as well.

The chapters that follow outline ways of thinking that we can use to familiarize our mind with patient acceptance.

Learning to Accept Suffering

There are three kinds of situation in which we need to learn to be patient: (1) when we are experiencing suffering, hardship or disappointment, (2) when we are practicing Dharma and (3) when we are harmed or criticized by others. Correspondingly, there are three types of patience: (1) the patience of voluntarily accepting suffering, (2) the patience of definitely thinking about Dharma and (3) the patience of not retaliating. These three types of patience do not come easily and may seem somewhat strange when we first read about them. However, once we understand them clearly and put them into practice sincerely and skillfully, they will liberate our mind from one of its most obsessive delusions and bring great peace and joy. It is therefore worthwhile to persevere in these practices even if initially they may seem unusual or even unnatural.

To practice the first patience—accepting willingly whatever suffering we cannot avoid—we should remember that, wherever we find ourself within samsara, only a few circumstances bring happiness whereas the causes of misery abound. This is the very nature of samsara—its sufferings are infinite while its joys are limited. Moreover, all the suffering we encounter is the result of actions we ourself have done in the past. If we do not experience this suffering, then who should? We should therefore learn to accept what is unavoidable rather than fight against it.

If we learn to accept unavoidable suffering, unhappy thoughts will never arise to disturb us. There are many difficult and unpleasant circumstances that we cannot avoid, but we can certainly avoid the unhappiness and anger these circumstances normally provoke in us. It is these habitual reactions to hardship, rather than the hardship itself, that disturb our day-to-day peace of mind, as well as our spiritual practice.

When we learn to accept difficult circumstances patiently, the real problem disappears. For example, suppose our body is afflicted by a painful illness. If we have a way of accepting the pain—for instance, by seeing it as a means of exhausting negative karma—our mind will remain at peace even though our body is in pain. Moreover, since physical pain is closely related to the tension and stress in our mind, as our mind relaxes we may discover that the physical pain actually subsides and our body is able to heal itself. However, if we refuse to deal realistically with the discomfort, cursing our illness and letting ourself become depressed, then not only will we have to endure the additional suffering of mental torment, but very probably our physical pain will increase as well.

Therefore we can see that responding to hardship with non-acceptance and anger only makes things worse. By destroying the merit, or positive potential, in our mind, anger makes it very difficult to fulfill our wishes; and by causing us to engage in negative actions, it sows the seeds for greater suffering in the future. In short, anger destroys our present peace and happiness, robs us of our future happiness and ensures that we suffer in life after life.

There are many benefits to be gained from patiently accepting suffering. Not only does it enable us to maintain a peaceful and positive mind in the face of distressing circumstances, but it also helps us to gain a clear and dispassionate view of the nature of our samsaric situation. There is a certain mental stability

When we learn to accept difficult circumstances patiently, the real problem disappears.

to be had merely from recognizing that every experience of pain or discomfort is the fault of our being caught up in samsara—of our being born, living and dying in a state of unknowing and confusion.

Our real problem is not the physical sickness, difficult relationship or financial hardship that we might currently be experiencing, but our being trapped in samsara. This recognition is the basis for developing renunciation, the spontaneous wish to attain complete freedom from every trace of dissatisfaction, which in turn is the foundation of all the higher spiritual realizations leading to the boundless happiness of liberation and enlightenment. But this recognition can only dawn within the clear and open mind of patient acceptance. For as long as we are in conflict with life's difficulties, thinking that things should be different from the way they are and blaming circumstances or other people for our unhappiness, we will never have the clarity or spaciousness of mind to see what it is that is really binding us. Patience allows us to see clearly the habit patterns that keep us locked in samsara, and thereby enables us to begin to undo them. Patience is therefore the foundation of the everlasting freedom and bliss of liberation.

Normally our need to escape from unpleasant feelings is so urgent that we do not give ourself the time to discover where these feelings actually come from. Suppose that someone we have helped responds with ingratitude, or that our partner fails to return our affection or that a colleague or boss continuously tries to belittle us and undermine our confidence. These things hurt, and our instinctive reaction is to try immediately to escape the painful feelings in our mind by becoming defensive, blaming the other person, retaliating or simply hardening our heart. Unfortunately, by reacting so quickly we do not give ourself the time to see what is actually going on in our mind. In reality, the painful feelings that arise on such occasions are not intolerable. They are only feelings, a few moments of bad weather in the mind, with no power to cause us any lasting harm. There is no need to take them so seriously. We are just one person among countless living beings, and a few moments of unpleasant feeling arising in the mind of just one person is no great catastrophe.

Just as there is room in the sky for a thunderstorm,

so there is room in the vast space of our mind for a few painful feelings; and just as a storm has no power to destroy the sky, so unpleasant feelings have no power to destroy our mind. When painful feelings arise in our mind, there is no need to panic; we can patiently accept them, experience them and investigate their nature and where they come from. When we do this, we will discover that painful feelings do not come to us from outside but arise from within our own mind. Circumstances or other people have no power to make us feel bad; the most they can do is trigger the potentials for painful feelings that already exist within our own mind. These potentials, or karmic imprints, are the residue of the negative actions we created in the past, which we performed because our mind was under the control of delusions, all of which stem from self-grasping ignorance. By patiently accepting painful feelings without clinging to them, the negative karmic potentials from which they arose are purified, and we will never have to experience that karma again.

Moreover, painful feelings can only arise and remain in our mind because of our present self-grasping. If we examine our mind carefully while we are experiencing painful emotions, we will discover that these feelings are invariably mixed with self-grasping. In particular, it is our grasping at an inherently existent I and mine that makes us suffer. The feelings of hurt are inseparably bound up with grasping at I and mine; we strongly feel "I am hurt" or "My feelings are hurt." The intensity of our suffering is in direct proportion to the intensity of our self-grasping.

We cannot immediately stop self-grasping, but if we stand back from the problem just enough to glimpse how self-grasping is creating the problem, the strength of our self-grasping is undermined.

There is an enormous difference between the thoughts "I am feeling bad" and "Unpleasant feelings are arising in my mind." When we identify with our feelings, we make them bigger and more solid than they are, and it becomes far more difficult to let the unpleasant feelings go. On the other hand, when we learn to view our feelings in a more detached way, seeing them simply as waves in the ocean of our mind, they become less frightening and much easier to deal with constructively.

We should not be discouraged by the difficulties involved in practicing patience. In ancient India, there were ascetics who endured tremendous pain and self-mortification merely to propitiate certain deities, and nowadays there are many athletes, dancers, models, soldiers and so forth who inflict extraordinary physical punishment upon themselves

When we identify with our feelings, we make them bigger and more solid than they are.

in the pursuit of their professions. It is easy to think of many other people who voluntarily endure great suffering merely to earn money or enhance their reputation. If they can bear such tremendous difficulties for limited goals, why can we not accept the difficulties and inconvenience involved in our pursuit of the ultimate happiness of enlightenment and the welfare of all living beings? Surely such a goal should be worth a little discomfort? Why are we so easily discouraged by the small difficulties of human life?

By familiarizing our mind with the patience of voluntarily accepting suffering, our problems and troubles will eventually disappear. Everything depends upon familiarity; once we are familiar with something we can accomplish it without any difficulty. If we do not learn to accept the comparatively small harms we experience in daily life, we will have to face far greater suffering in the future. On the other hand, if we learn to be patient with relatively minor sufferings, such as criticism, unpopularity and slander, we will gradually learn to cope with greater sufferings and pains. Eventually we will be able to accept with a calm and happy mind all the sufferings of human life, such as heat, cold, hunger, thirst, disease, imprisonment, physical abuse and even death. In this way, we will be able to live without fear, knowing there is nothing that could happen to us that we cannot accept and transform into the spiritual path.

Shantideva gives an analogy to show how we can increase the strength of our patient acceptance. When a war-hardened soldier is wounded in battle and sees his own blood, the sight makes him roar defiantly and increases his courage and strength. On the other hand, a man unused to fighting is discouraged merely by the sight of another person's blood, perhaps becoming so weak that he even faints! Since both these men see human blood, why is the soldier encouraged and the other man discouraged? The difference is due to the force of familiarity. The more familiar we become with the patient acceptance of suffering, the more the strength of our patience will increase. Therefore, whenever we experience suffering we should recall the teachings on patience and thereby prevent this suffering from harming us.

Whenever a wise person intent on attaining enlightenment encounters difficulties or adverse conditions, he or she endures these without letting them disturb his peaceful mind. We should realize that our deadliest enemies are anger and the other delusions. Since these delusions are deeply ingrained mental habits, working to overcome them is not always easy. Anyone who has given up smoking or another addiction knows how hard it can be to go against the grain of our harmful habits. A certain amount of suffering is therefore inevitable in the course of our spiritual practice, but if we remind ourself of the limitless benefits of overcoming our negativity, this will not be too difficult to bear. After all, the suffering involved in overcoming our negativity pales into insignificance when compared with the suffering involved in not overcoming our negativity!

The person who bears all suffering and overcomes the enemies of anger and other delusions is truly worthy of being called a "hero" or "heroine." Usually we reserve this title for someone who kills other living beings in battle, but such a person is not really a hero because his enemy would have died naturally in the course of time anyway. What he did was not much different from killing a corpse. But our internal enemies—the delusions—will never die a natural death. If we do not exert effort in ridding our mind of these persistent foes, they will keep us locked in the prison of samsara, as they have done since beginningless time.

For developing spiritual realizations, suffering has many good qualities; so for a spiritual practitioner it need not be a negative experience. Through reflecting on our own suffering, we can develop many useful insights and positive qualities. Recognizing our vulnerability dispels our arrogance and deluded pride. Understanding how our present suffering is merely a symptom of our being in samsara enables us to develop renunciation. Furthermore, we can use our own pain to understand the pain of all living beings. Having learned to accept our own suffering patiently, if we then think of the suffering of all the other living beings trapped in samsara, compassion will arise naturally.

Renunciation and compassion are two of the most important spiritual realizations, and it is our suffering that enables us to gain these realizations. Those who do not learn to face with courage the truth of suffering, and to accept their own problems patiently, will not only feel helpless and unhappy but also deprive themselves of the opportunity to develop any authentic spiritual realizations.

Listen to the precious sound of the conch of Dharma
and contemplate and meditate on its meaning

The Patience of Definitely
Thinking About Dharma

Whenever we practice Dharma with a patient and joyful mind, we are practicing the patience of definitely thinking about Dharma. Such patience is necessary because if our mind is impatient or unhappy when we engage in spiritual practice, this will obstruct our spiritual progress and prevent us from improving our wisdom. Even if we find some aspects of our practice difficult, we still need to practice with a happy mind.

In *Guide to the Bodhisattva's Way of Life* Shantideva explains this patience from a slightly different angle. According to this explanation, we are practicing the patience of definitely thinking about Dharma whenever we use our understanding of profound Dharma instructions, such as those on emptiness or dependent relationship, in order to deepen our experience of patience.

This type of patience is important because the wisdom realizing emptiness is the only direct method of eradicating our delusions and suffering. If we use our experience of mental and physical suffering as an opportunity to improve our understanding of emptiness, not only will our pain become far more tolerable, but our experience of emptiness will also deepen considerably. Whenever we are suffering, our self-grasping generally manifests more strongly than normal. This makes our self-grasping easier to identify, thus helping our meditation on emptiness to make an unusually deep impact on our mind. Also, our pain forces us to look more carefully into the actual causes and nature of pain, pulling us deeper and deeper into the truth of emptiness.

When a person is afflicted by a disease such as cancer, he or she experiences great physical pain. What caused this pain? The disease. If someone hits us on the head with a stick, pain also arises. What caused this pain? The wielder of the stick. If pain is experienced in both cases, why are we more likely to get angry with the person who wielded the stick than with the disease?

The obvious answer is that it is not appropriate to generate anger toward a disease, because it does not choose to cause us suffering. A disease simply arises when all the causes and conditions for it to arise are assembled; it is not an independent agent that chooses to harm us. Because of this, anger is clearly not an appropriate response. Yet if we do not get angry with a disease, neither should we get angry with a person who harms us. Why? Because he too is not a free and independent agent—he acts solely under the power of his delusions. If we are to get angry at all, we should direct our anger at these delusions.

Just as we do not choose to suffer from sickness, so

the person who beats us does not choose to suffer from the inner sickness of anger. We might think that there is a difference between our sickness and the angry person, in that our sickness has no wish to harm us whereas an enemy most certainly does have this wish. What we must realize, however, is that the person who wishes to harm us does so without freedom; he is completely under the control of his anger. He does not decide, "Now I will become angry"; anger simply arises and takes over his mind without any choice on his part.

All shortcomings, delusions and non-virtues arise through the force of conditions; they do not govern themselves. The assembled conditions that cause suffering have no intention to produce suffering, and nor does the resultant suffering think, "I was produced by assembled conditions." Therefore, the angry person, the anger itself and the suffering that results from it are completely without independent existence; they exist solely in dependence upon their causes and conditions.

All things, including our state of mind, are dependent arisings; they do not have an independent or self-existent nature of their own. It is therefore senseless to react with anger toward people or situations that have no choice in causing us harm. If we train our mind to see the interdependent nature of all phenomena, we will be able to eliminate the cause of much of our anger.

Our normal view is that there is an inherently existent aggressor harming an inherently existent victim. This is a complete misconception of the situation. In reality, the aggressor and the victim are interdependent and utterly without inherent, or independent, existence. If we mentally try to isolate the aggressor from everything else in order to pinpoint someone we can blame, we cannot do so, because the aggressor has no existence independent of the other elements of the situation. The aggressor depends on his delusions and on the karma of the victim that impelled the aggressor to behave in that way at that moment; as well as on the circumstances of the situation, his personal and family background, the society in which he lives, his previous lives and his being trapped in a samsaric body and mind. When we search for the aggressor in this way, he disappears in an endless web of relationships, causes and conditions—there is no inherently existent person we can find to blame.

Pain ceases to exist when we discover its real nature.

In the same way, the delusion that motivated the attack, the attack itself, the victim and the victim's suffering are all completely unfindable. If we are attacked, we strongly feel that we are a victim, but if we search analytically for this victim, trying to isolate it from everything else, we will not find anything. There is nothing we can grasp onto as a victim; where we expected to find an inherently existent victim, we discover an emptiness that is the utter non-existence of such a victim. The victim is merely a label, a term in the conventional description of the event, existing in relation to all the other terms but not referring to anything real and findable. When we analyze the situation in this way, we discover that there is no one to blame and no one to feel sorry for. Everything disappears into an equal, undifferentiated emptiness, which is the true nature of all things.

It is also very helpful to examine the real nature of our pain. What precisely is pain? Where is it located? What is it made of? Where does it come from? Where does it go to? What relation does it have to us—the person who is in pain—or to the mind that is asking these questions? Pain naturally appears to us as something solid and undeniably real—something inherently existent—but when we search for it analytically, trying mentally to isolate pain from everything that is not pain, we cannot find it. Pain has no independent, concrete existence. This lack of inherent existence, or emptiness, is the real nature of pain. In emptiness there is no pain. Pain is merely an appearance to mind, existing only for a mind that does not see its real nature. Just as a mirage in a desert disappears when we search for it, so pain ceases to exist when we discover its real nature.

All effects arise from causes, and these causes also arise from previous causes. Since all causes and effects arise in dependence upon other causes and conditions, they completely lack any independent, or inherent, existence. Even though all things seem to exist from their own side, they are in reality like illusions. If we can remember to look at things in this light whenever difficulties present themselves, our anger and indeed all our delusions will vanish. Keeping such thoughts in mind when encountering anger-provoking situations is part of practicing the patience of definitely thinking about Dharma.

It might be argued that if everything is like an illusion, who is there who should restrain what anger? All such restraint would be inappropriate in a world of illusions. This is a misunderstanding. Although things are like illusions in that they lack self-existence, suffering is still experienced. Overcoming this suffering depends upon making an effort to restrain delusions such as our anger. Although things lack independent existence—in fact *because* they lack independent existence—cause and effect operate to bring suffering results from non-virtuous actions and beneficial results from virtuous actions. Therefore, it is never appropriate to indulge in anger, because this only plants the seeds for future misery.

When we are about to get angry, we should analyze the situation. We can ask ourself, "Who is there to get angry? Who is there to restrain what anger?" In this way, we will find that in reality there is no one to get angry and no anger to restrain. As a result our anger will disappear. Ultimately there is no anger, no object of anger and no one who gets angry. Conventionally, however, anger exists and produces suffering, and so it needs to be restrained.

In summary, whenever we are harmed by anyone, we should think, "It is only because of his delusion that this person is harming me; he does not act freely." If in this way we can realize that all things arise from causes and conditions, we can prevent anger and remain in a happy state of mind no matter what happens.

If everything that arose did so according to its own independent, free choice, sentient beings would never have to experience any suffering, because no one would choose to suffer and everyone would choose to be happy all the time. Clearly there must be another explanation for why we suffer. We do not suffer because we choose to suffer, but because our mind is controlled by self-grasping ignorance. Since beginningless time, our mind has been governed by self-grasping, which prevents us from seeing things as they really are and causes us to engage in all kinds of unskillful and inappropriate actions. It is because of this that sentient beings suffer and cause others to suffer, not because they freely choose to do so. When we understand this deeply, we will never feel anger toward sentient beings. Instead of anger, compassion will arise naturally in our hearts.

Apply great effort to attain enlightenment

Learning Not to Retaliate

We have already discussed the many visible and invisible faults of anger, but how can we stop wanting to retaliate when someone harms us? The best way to overcome our instinctive desire to retaliate is to combine patient acceptance with compassion. When someone harms us, we should not only think, "He is hurting me only because he is deluded," but also, "He is hurting himself, too." Through training our mind to see things in this way, compassion will spontaneously arise and all impulses toward anger and retaliation will subside.

The ways in which people bring harm to themselves are numerous and varied. In their search for sexual partners, wealth or social position, some people become so obsessed that they deprive themselves of food, almost starving themselves to death. Overcome by greed or anger, people even murder their parents, destroying any hope for a happy life for themselves in the process. When we look around us or read the newspapers, we can see innumerable examples of how, through their delusions, people inflict untold suffering upon themselves. Delusions are completely merciless and benefit no one, least of all the people who fall under their control. When we think of the immediate and future harm their delusions inflict upon these people, we can better understand why they often harm us as well. If we contemplate this deeply, not only will we overcome the wish to retaliate, but we will also be able to generate compassion for those who harm us.

Under the influence of anger, a person who normally cherishes himself more than anything else in the world is even capable of committing suicide. If the force of his delusions can drive him to such desperate measures, we can certainly see how it can cause him to inflict pain on others. Anger can so totally rob a person of his or her freedom of action that it is unreasonable for us to express hostility toward anyone under its sway. If we cannot generate compassion for such an unfortunate person, at the very least we should try to refrain from getting angry with him.

Remember at all times that anger is everyone's principal enemy.

The capacity to remain completely unruffled in situations of great provocation, and to feel genuine compassion for those who are deliberately trying to harm us, is a sign of high spiritual realizations and the result of a great deal of mental preparation. It is unrealistic to expect that we can immediately be like this, but, if we use every opportunity that arises in our daily life to train our mind in the following methods for controlling our anger, our patience will gradually improve. Occasionally, of course, our old habits of anger will get the better of us, but we should not become discouraged by this. If we persevere, little by little we will certainly gain control over our anger. Finally we will reach the point where we no longer need to make an effort not to get angry—anger will simply no longer be a natural response to hardship or provocation.

The first thing we need to do is to remember at all times that anger is everyone's principal enemy. Anger is the friend of no one. Our anger never helps us, and another person's anger never helps them. All anger ever does is destroy our own and others' virtues and bring nothing but unhappiness. One of the effects of acting out of anger is that in the future, whether we are reborn as a human being or otherwise, our body will be ugly. There are certain people and animals who instinctively arouse fear and loathing in others. Being reborn with such a repulsive form, as well as being disliked by others and having a temperament that is quick to anger, are all karmic results of an angry mind. On the other hand, an attractive body and a pleasing appearance are the karmic results of the practice of patience.

Having recognized anger as our main enemy, we should then make a strong decision not to allow it to arise. By remembering this decision in our daily life, we should stop ourself from getting angry. This might sound easier said than done, but if we now make a firm decision not to get angry for the rest of the day, or at least until the next mealtime, the chances are that we will succeed. Then, if we can succeed for one day, we can succeed for two days, then three days, then a week and so on for the rest of our life. Abandoning all our anger is a big job, but if we take it one step at a time it is not so difficult, and gradually the tendencies of anger in our mind will become weaker and weaker.

When we are harmed by another person, we should examine whether it is his or her essential nature to be harmful or whether this is just a temporary fault. If it were true that being harmful was the very nature of this person, there really would be no reason to become angry with him. We do not blame fire when we are burned by it because we know that it is the very nature of fire to burn. In the same way, if it is this person's very nature to be harmful, then there is nothing he can do about it and so there is no point in being angry with him.

On the other hand, if the harmfulness of our aggressor is only a temporary fault, arising in response to changing circumstances, there is also no reason for us to become angry with him. When too much rain falls from the sky we do not become angry with the sky, because we realize that rain is not part of its essential nature. Rain falls from the sky only as the result of temporary circumstances such as temperature, humidity and air pressure. Therefore, if the harmfulness of our aggressor is not part of his essential nature, whose fault is it that he harms us? It is the fault of his delusion.

Let us imagine that an angry man picks up a stick and hits us with it. Surely it is right to get angry with this man—after all, this man has harmed us! Now suppose a friend tries to restrain us by saying, "Don't get angry with the man, get angry with the stick! It's the stick that was the immediate cause of your pain." It is unlikely that such an argument would convince us. We would almost certainly retort, "The stick didn't hit me by itself. Without the man who wielded it, it would have had no power to hurt me. It's the man I should be angry with."

If this line of reasoning keeps us from getting angry at the stick, we should apply it to the man as well. The man was manipulated by his anger in exactly the same way that the stick was manipulated by the man. With scarcely any control over his mind, he was at the mercy of his delusions. Therefore, if being harmed is going to provoke anger in us at all, we should direct our wrath against the actual cause of our pain—the delusion of anger itself. Wrath directed at a person's delusions—once we have clearly differentiated the person from his or her delusions and recognized the person as a victim of his delusions—is not actual anger but a forceful form of compassion. Our wish is to protect the person from his inner enemy of anger, and we use whatever means are available to us, whether gentle or forceful, to free him from this delusion.

It is important to understand that when we practice the patience of not retaliating we are mainly concerned with our own internal, mental reaction to experiences of pain and discomfort. No suggestion is being made that we should passively let ourself be beaten or harmed merely for the sake of practicing patience. If there is a way for us to prevent someone from hurting both us and himself, then certainly we should do so. However, the question here is, "What should I do with my mind once I have already been harmed?" The entire practice of patience, and indeed of Buddha's teachings as a whole, is to provide protection for the mind. Ultimately it is our mind that determines whether we are happy or miserable.

Another powerful method for overcoming anger and the wish to retaliate is to see all undesirable situations as a reflection of our own faults and shortcomings. If someone insults us, for instance, we can remember the teachings on karma and think, "I would not be suffering this harm now if I had not insulted someone similarly in the past." We can use the same approach in regard to sickness, injury or any other problem. Our ability to think in this way depends upon our understanding and familiarity with the teachings on the law of karma. Once we have firm conviction in karma and realize that we always reap the results of our own actions, receiving good for good and evil for evil, we will be able to remain inwardly peaceful and calm even in the most adverse circumstances. We can view the harm we receive with a sense of relief, seeing our pain as the repayment of a long-standing debt. This is certainly preferable to becoming angry and upset, which only incurs the future debt of more pain and anguish.

Shantideva suggests that whenever someone harms us physically, we should remember that there are two immediate causes of the suffering we experience: the weapon used against us, and our own body. Since it is only when these two factors meet that suffering arises, at which should we direct our anger? If we direct it at our attacker or the weapon he or she uses, why do we not similarly direct it at our own body? On the other hand, if we never direct anger at our own body, why do we direct it at the attacker and his weapon?

To make sense of this argument, we need to understand why it is that we have a body that can so easily be harmed and is so prone to discomfort and pain. Our human body is described as a "contaminated body" because it is the result of contaminated causes. In previous lives, lacking wisdom and driven by self-grasping ignorance and craving, we created the karma to take on the contaminated human body we now have. It is the nature of a contaminated body to give rise to suffering, just as it is the nature of an old car to break down. Once we take on a contaminated body, physical suffering is inevitable. If we wish to avoid physical suffering in the future, we need to create the karma to obtain a pure, uncontaminated body. Just as a contaminated body arises from impure karma created out of self-grasping ignorance, so an uncontaminated body arises from pure karma created within a direct realization of selflessness. Until we obtain an uncontaminated body, however, we need to accept that physical suffering is inevitable. Rather than blaming

Ultimately it is our mind that determines whether we are happy or miserable.

temporary conditions such as thorns or weapons for our pain, we should recognize that the basis of all our physical pain and discomfort is our contaminated body, which we have taken as a result of our own past actions.

We all wish for happiness and freedom from suffering, but controlled by our delusions of attachment, anger and so forth, we think nothing of creating the causes that lead to suffering. All the harm we receive is the result of the deluded actions that we ourself have created, and so it is completely inappropriate to blame this suffering on others. What reason, then, is there for us to become angry?

All the sufferings of samsara, even those of the deepest hell, are produced by our own actions. The torments of hell are not punishments imposed from outside by a god or a demon but the creation of the severely disturbed minds of those who are suffering these torments. In the same way, the suffering we experience now is not imposed on us from outside but is solely the result of our own negative karma. Even when another person attacks us, it is our karma that impels him to behave in that way. The other person is merely the instrument of our karma, and if harm had not reached us through him, it would certainly reach us in some other way. Other people are not to blame for our suffering. The only things we can blame are our own delusions and negative actions. If we wish to avoid experiencing unbearable suffering, the only appropriate course of action is to abandon all our delusions and faults in this very life. Once we gain control over our mind in this way, there is nothing in samsara to fear.

We should be careful not to misunderstand this teaching on blaming our delusions. Our delusions and negative actions are to blame for everything that goes wrong in our lives, but this does not mean that we are to blame. We are the victim of our delusions, and it is unfair to blame a victim for the faults of his or her attacker. For example, if someone steals from us, this is the karmic result of an action of stealing we performed in a previous life and thus the fault of our delusions and deluded actions, but it is clearly not the fault of the person we are now. It is not even the fault of the person we were then, because that person was only acting under the control of his delusions. It makes no sense to blame ourself for the problems and suffering we now experience. Yet although it is not our fault that we experience suffering, it is nevertheless our responsibility to accept the disagreeable consequences of our previous negative actions and deal with them constructively.

Another way to help us overcome our wish to retaliate is to investigate closely who actually suffers and who benefits when we receive harm from someone else. When someone becomes angry with us and causes us harm, we serve as the object provoking his or her anger. If we were not there, his anger would not have arisen. Why did he get angry with us? It is rare that people are angry with us totally out of the blue—there is almost always something we did to cause offense that served as an

[margin note: Negative experiences & interactions when we are attacked, criticized, embarassed are opportunities to clear our bad karma + create good karma IF HANDLED WITH PATIENT ACCEPTANCE]

immediate condition to trigger their anger. But even if we did nothing, at a deeper level it was the ripening of our previous negative karma that created the situation in which it was natural for them to get angry with and harm us. The harm we receive is therefore the ripening of our own past actions, not the fault of the other person, and so we should accept it patiently. If we do this, not only will we remain at peace now, but we will also become free of that particular negative karma. The other person has actually helped us to purify our negative karma and to create the immensely positive karma of patient acceptance. Looked at in this way, the person who harmed us can be seen as the source of our happiness. If we step outside our narrow view and take a comprehensive look at what is actually happening, we will understand that his harmful actions can in fact be a source of great benefit to us.

What does our attacker gain from getting angry and harming us? Because we provided an object for his anger, he will find unhappiness in this life and plant the seeds for a future lower rebirth. In fact, therefore, we have harmed him and he has benefited us! If this is so, why should we become angry with him? By harming us he has allowed us to practice patience, helping us to purify our past negativity and to create great merit. On the other hand, what have we done for him? By serving as his object of anger, we have allowed him to create much non-virtue, impelling him toward the lower realms. To become angry with such an unfortunate, ill-destined benefactor is surely the behavior of a confused mind!

If our true goal in life is the everlasting peace and joy of liberation and full enlightenment, material wealth is of little consequence. Only the internal wealth of virtue is of real importance. The enemy who allows us to practice patience and thereby accumulate an inexhaustible wealth of virtue is a treasure trove of incalculable value. Without him, how could we develop the virtuous mind of patience? Whenever we are harmed, abused, criticized and so forth, the opportunity arises to create immense inner wealth. The person who harms us, therefore, should be seen for what he really is—an ally and benefactor who fulfills all our wishes.

The practice of non-retaliation goes against our deeply ingrained habit patterns, so it is not surprising if our mind comes up with many objections to it. Shantideva anticipates and answers some of these objections as follows.

Even if I practice patience when someone harms me, won't I be reborn in the lower realms for acting as his object of anger?
The answer is no. If we contemplate how an enemy is of benefit to us, and practice patience with the harm he or she causes, we will not be accumulating any non-virtue. Since we have not created a non-virtuous cause we will not experience a suffering result.

In that case the person who harms me will also not receive suffering results from his action, since he created the beneficial circumstances for my practice of patience.
This is also not true. Karmic results are experienced only

by the person who performed the action. There is no way for the person who harms us to receive the fruit of our virtuous practice of patience. Because his actions were not virtuous, how can he obtain a happy result from them?

Then perhaps if someone harms me the best thing I could do is retaliate, since I will then be the object of his patience and therefore of benefit to him?

There are several reasons why this is a mistaken notion. First of all, if we retaliate to harm we will be damaging our own spiritual development, weakening our bodhichitta and causing our practice of patience to degenerate. Secondly, there is no certainty at all that if we retaliate to the harm we receive our adversary will practice patience. Since he is already in an angry frame of mind, it is far more likely that he will only react with more anger. Even if he did practice patience, this would not keep our own spiritual practice from degenerating.

There is a good reason for becoming angry and retaliating when someone harms my body. My body experiences suffering, and because my mind strongly holds onto this body as its own, it is therefore appropriate for my mind to become upset and wish to retaliate.

This line of reasoning is illogical. If it were true, then why do we get angry when someone speaks harshly to us? These unpleasant, empty words do not have the power from their own side to harm our body or our mind, so why do we wish to retaliate?

I should retaliate because other people hearing these harsh and slanderous words will dislike me.

Even if they do, the dislike they might feel toward us has absolutely no power to bring us harm either in this life or in future lives. So there is no reason to become upset.

If people dislike me and I receive a bad reputation, this will prevent me from obtaining a good position and wealth. To avoid this, I must retaliate to the harm I receive.

If we retaliate to harm and abandon the practice of patience, we will create even greater obstacles to our pursuit of position and wealth. The practice of patience never hinders such attainments; in fact, it helps us to achieve them. If we do not retaliate to harm, we will naturally receive a good reputation, a respected position and wealth, either in this life or in future lives.

Furthermore, there is absolutely no purpose in generating anger in our pursuit of material gain, because no matter how much we might acquire, it will all be left behind when we die. All that will remain and travel with us into the future are the imprints of the anger that we have placed upon our consciousness. It is far better to die today than to live a long life full of negative actions.

No matter how long we live, it is certain that one day we will all die. If one person dreams of enjoying one hundred years of happiness, and another dreams of enjoying one moment of happiness, when they wake up their dream experiences amount to the same thing—nothing is left of either. In a similar manner, whether we live a long and pleasant life or a short and difficult life, when we die it amounts to the same—the only thing that will help us is the strength of our virtuous actions. Even though we may live a long and full life, enjoying all the wealth and pleasures this world has to offer, when death comes it will be like being robbed by a thief. We will go empty-handed and naked into the future.

Is it not important for me to acquire material wealth now so that I can support my life and thereby have the opportunity to purify my negativities and accumulate merit?
As stated before, if in our quest for material wealth we spend our life committing non-virtue, and thereby allow our virtuous qualities to degenerate, there is no purpose at all in living for a long time.

Perhaps I should not retaliate if a person hinders me from accumulating material wealth, but if he or she damages my reputation I should certainly retaliate, or else those who have faith in me will lose it.
Yet if we retaliate when we ourself are verbally abused, why do we not retaliate when someone else is the object of verbal abuse? Does this not cause other people to lose faith in him as well? It makes no sense to be patient when someone else is abused but impatient when we are the object of abuse. All abuse arises from mistaken conceptions and therefore there is no reason to respond to it with anger. Besides, do we really think that people's faith in us will increase through seeing us retaliate?

Perhaps I can practice patience if I alone am the object of harm, but if someone abuses the Three Jewels, as a Buddhist I should certainly retaliate. Surely there can be no fault in this?

The Buddhas are completely beyond all harm, and so it is inappropriate to generate anger toward someone even if he or she insults the Three Jewels, destroys holy images or denigrates Dharma in any other way. It is clear that anyone committing such senseless actions must be completely under the power of his or her delusions. Such a powerless being should be the object not of our anger but of our compassion.

Even if those who are close to us, such as our Spiritual Guide, family and friends, are harmed, we should still refrain from retaliating or becoming angry. We should realize that all such harm is the ripening of past deeds. Of course, if it is within our power we should certainly try to prevent others from causing harm, but we should do so out of love and compassion rather than out of anger. Practicing patience does not mean that we should let others commit non-virtue without intervening—it only means that we should guard our own mind from the delusion of anger.

The harm we receive comes from two sources—animate and inanimate objects—so why is it that our anger is particularly generated toward animate objects? If we are patient with one type of harm, we can certainly learn to be patient with the other. Moreover, if one person out of ignorance harms someone else, and the latter out of ignorance becomes angry with him, who is at fault and who is without fault? Whether it is hurting someone out of anger or retaliating to the harm with anger, both actions arise from the confusion of ignorance. To respond to either with anger is therefore illogical.

Everything we experience is dependent on causes and conditions. Both our antagonist and we ourself have created the karma to interact in the way we have done. It is not a case of a guilty aggressor harming an innocent victim, because the aggressor and victim are both caught up in the same unfortunate karmic scenario. Therefore, there is never any reason for us to bear malice toward our enemies. Once we have seen the truth of this, we should work toward the happiness of everyone, and generate the wish that all living beings learn to live harmoniously, with love for one another.

Pure love unmixed with attachment does not lead to anger.

Attachment to loved ones is a common cause of our anger because we often retaliate on their behalf. If one house is on fire, the dry grass around it can easily spread the fire to other houses, which then consumes these houses and everything in them. In a similar fashion, when those we cling to are harmed, the dry grass of attachment carries their harm to us, igniting in us the fire of anger, which consumes our wealth of merit. To prevent this from happening, we should not create objects of attachment.

In samsara all meetings lead to partings, and everything that comes together is eventually torn apart. Whether we are attached to our family and friends or not, we will eventually be separated from them, either before death or by death. Since separation is an inevitable part of a samsaric human rebirth, we should be prepared to accept it. In *Guide to the Bodhisattva's Way of Life* Shantideva gives the example of a prisoner who is about to be executed, but, due to the intervention of others, is pardoned and sentenced instead to having his hand cut off. Even though he has to experience the suffering of losing his hand, he will certainly rejoice and feel very fortunate that his life has been spared. In a similar way, a person experiencing the sufferings of the human realm, such as those of being separated from objects of attachment, should consider himself fortunate that he is spared the far worse miseries of lower realms.

Giving up objects of attachment means that we should give up the delusion of attachment we have in our mind toward our family and friends. It does not mean that we should give up our relationships with our loved ones or refuse to help them when they are in trouble. In general, it is important to maintain and improve our relationships with our close circle, but there is no point in getting angry on their behalf. When we are attached to someone, we need him to make us happy, but when he is in pain or difficulty he does not function properly to provide us with the happiness we want from him. This is why we get angry when he is harmed. Pure love unmixed with attachment, however, does not lead to anger. When someone we love, but for whom we have no attachment, is harmed, a powerful desire to protect and help him arises in our hearts; but we feel no anger toward his aggressor. We take whatever practical steps we can to defend our friend, but we have no desire at all to make the aggressor suffer. What we need to do, therefore, is give up our attachment to our loved ones, but never give up our love.

Even if I can learn to bear the suffering of separation, I cannot bear the pain of abuse and slander!
If we cannot bear this relatively slight suffering, how will we ever be able to endure the unbearable sufferings of the lower realms? Yet if we cannot bear the sufferings of lower realms, why do we continue to become angry and thereby create the causes for such unfortunate rebirths? In the past, because of our confusion about the law of karma and because our mind was polluted by the poisons of anger and attachment, we experienced immense suffering in these realms, but none of this suffering brought us any benefit. Now that we have obtained this precious human life, however, we have the unique opportunity to make our suffering meaningful by transforming it into the spiritual path. By accepting the comparatively insignificant suffering we experience in the human realm, and using it to increase our renunciation, compassion and other spiritual realizations, we can quickly attain the supreme happiness of full enlightenment and become of benefit to all living beings. Realizing this, we should willingly accept whatever hardships we may encounter with a happy and peaceful mind.

Anger is often related to jealousy and so we need to

try to overcome both these delusions. When a rival is successful or praised, it is very easy to feel jealous, but why should someone else's happiness make us unhappy? If we step out of our egocentric view for a moment and put ourself in the other person's place, instead of feeling the pain of jealousy we can rejoice and share in his or her happiness.

When a jealous person sees signs of other people's success and good fortune, his heart is pierced with envy; but someone who has learned to rejoice in the good fortune of others experiences only happiness. Seeing another person's beautiful house or attractive partner immediately makes him happy; the fact that they are not his own is irrelevant. When he sees a colleague praised or promoted, or when he meets someone who is more intelligent, good-looking or successful than him, instead of immediately being reminded of his own inadequacies he simply shares in the other person's happiness.

Rejoicing in other people's happiness or good qualities is one of the purest of all virtuous minds, because it is unstained by self-cherishing. When we practice giving, for example, it is possible that we might hope for something in return—for gratitude, to be liked or to be thought of as a generous person—but when we rejoice in another's good fortune we expect nothing in return.

Rejoicing in the good fortune of others creates the cause for us to enjoy similar good fortune in the future, and rejoicing in the good qualities of others creates the cause for us to develop similar qualities. It is said that those who now appreciate and rejoice in the good qualities of spiritual practitioners and realized beings will become pure spiritual practitioners in their next life. Rejoicing is the easiest way to increase our merit, it delights all the Buddhas and it is the supreme method for gathering a circle of friends.

If seeing others happy displeases us, it follows that we should not pay wages to those who work for us because this makes them happy. Yet we know full well that if we do not pay these wages, our employees will refuse to work and so our own present and future happiness will diminish. Rejoicing in the praise that others receive is similar to paying fair wages, because this is both pleasing to them and in our own best interest.

When someone praises us and talks about our good qualities, we become happy. Since everyone else also enjoys receiving such praise, we should be happy when this happens too. It is only our senseless jealousy that deprives us of feeling pleasure when others receive praise. It is particularly absurd for those who have generated bodhichitta to feel jealous. If we have the aspiration to benefit all living beings, why should we ever become unhappy when, through their own efforts, others find a small measure of happiness? Since we have promised to lead all living beings to the state of Buddhahood—a state in which they will receive worship and praise from countless beings—why do we begrudge them the temporary pleasures they find now? To become angry with them in this way is ridiculous!

Parents are responsible for the welfare of their children, but when the children are eventually able to look after themselves and earn their own living the parents are pleased. They are happy at their children's accomplishment and feel no jealousy. In a similar way, if we wish to lead all living beings to fortunate states of existence, liberation and enlightenment, there is no reason to become jealous and angry when they find a little happiness for themselves. If, instead, we do become jealous on such occasions, how can we claim to be practicing the Bodhisattva's way of life? As long as our mind is filled with jealousy, we will never be able to develop the precious heart of bodhichitta. When jealousy, hatred and the other delusions arise, our bodhichitta automatically degenerates. If we are truly interested in following a path that leads to enlightenment, we should do everything in our power to defeat these delusions quickly and completely.

Jealousy is one of the most senseless and purposeless of all the delusions. Nothing can be gained from being jealous of another's good fortune, good job, reputation or success. Suppose someone gives a rival some money. The jealousy and unhappiness we feel about this will do nothing to change the situation. Whether our rival is given money or not, there is no way in which we are going to receive that money ourself. So why should we be jealous? Furthermore, developing jealousy on the one hand yet wishing to obtain wealth and possessions on the other, are contradictory states of mind. Why? The root cause of receiving wealth, possessions and any other pleasurable things is our own accumulation of virtue, which is created by giving, rejoicing, appreciating and respecting others and so forth. However, when due to our self-centered view of the world strong jealousy arises in our mind, the potentialities of these virtuous actions are damaged and so our chances to experience good fortune in the future are diminished or destroyed. Therefore, if we really wish to obtain good fortune, wealth and so forth in the future, we should guard our mind well, and instead of allowing jealousy to arise toward others' happiness, we should rejoice.

There is also no reason to be happy when our enemy meets with suffering, because how do such negative thoughts either hurt our enemy or benefit us? Even if we were to think, "How wonderful it would be if my rival were to suffer," this would never harm him or her. And even if he were harmed, how would that ever bring us happiness?

But if my enemy suffers, I will be satisfied.
Thoughts like this never bring us any happiness. On the contrary, nothing harms us more than indulging in such petty and vengeful thoughts, which do nothing but drag us down into the lower realms.

If I do not retaliate when others harm me, what will people think? Will my fame, reputation and praise not decrease?
Although one of the main reasons we retaliate is to defend our reputation, in reality we can actually protect

and enhance our reputation far more effectively by practicing patience. When people see that we have the strength and stability of character to absorb criticism, slander and abuse without losing our poise and good humor, their respect for us will increase. When a movie star or politician takes offense at a petty criticism and immediately sues for libel, does our respect for him increase? Probably we would respect him more if he took himself less seriously and could weather a little criticism without losing his dignity or peace of mind. Patience is a strength, not a weakness; and if by practicing patience we stop retaliating to harm and criticism, people will gradually come to understand that our real nature is very special.

Praise and reputation are not worth getting angry and upset about. It is true that a good reputation, wealth and a respected position in society are generally quite beneficial, and like all experiences of pleasure they are the result of our own skillful

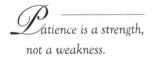

Patience is a strength, not a weakness.

and virtuous actions of the past. Yet if our attachment to these fortunate conditions forces us to become angry when they are threatened, they cease to be beneficial and instead become just more causes of suffering. We should understand that it is not good external circumstances in themselves that make us happy, but the way our mind relates to them. Anyone who has even an inkling of how far the mind can be developed will never be satisfied with insubstantial attainments. Therefore, we should abandon attachment to these things, and having obtained this precious human form, practice the essence of Dharma and remove delusions from our mind. How can we allow our attachment to the insignificant pleasure a few words of praise can give us to get in the way of our finding the limitless bliss of enlightenment?

For the sake of fame and reputation some people sacrifice large amounts of money and even their life, but what is the value of sacrificing so much for a few dry, empty words? Who benefits if we die in the process of seeking fame and glory? Those who become elated when praised, or miserable and angry when criticized, were referred to by Buddha as "the childish." Children at the beach love to make sandcastles, but when the surf eventually sweeps these piles of sand away, they cry with disappointment, "My castle is gone!" Similarly, if we allow our mind to be swept here and there by the changing waves of praise and criticism, we are as foolish as these children.

Although there is no sense in becoming angry or upset when we are criticized or slandered, there are times when it may be necessary to defend our reputation by explaining the truth. Suppose a politician with a sincere wish to serve the people is falsely accused of faults and misdemeanors. If he or she does not take steps to defend himself, he may risk losing his position and with it the chance to help many people. Realizing this, there is no fault if, without anger or the wish to retaliate, he explains to the public that these accusations are completely unfounded.

When the mere sound of a few words of praise reaches our ears, why do we become so happy? After all, the sound itself has no mind, and no intention to praise us.

Since the person who praises me is happy to do so, I should also be happy.
But his pleasure is entirely in his own mind and benefits us neither now nor in the future.

Yet it is right to be pleased at another's pleasure. You have just said that we should rejoice when others are happy.
This is very true, and we should familiarize our mind with this attitude until we can rejoice even upon seeing our rival's happiness. It is senseless to have the falsely discriminating mind that is pleased when our friends are praised but jealous when our enemies are. Moreover, to savor the praise that we ourself receive is like the behavior of a small child.

Although a good reputation, a high position and wealth are generally considered beneficial, they can in fact hinder our attainment of enlightenment by distracting our untamed mind from the spiritual path. As a result of focusing on our reputation and the like, our renunciation can easily decline, and pride, competitiveness and jealousy can arise. Such distractions cause our own virtues to decrease and interrupt our ability to help others. Through being attached to a good reputation and so forth, we will descend to the lower realms and remain caught in the swamp of samsara.

A person who is trying to practice Dharma purely

is better off without these obstacles and distractions. Who helps us break our attachment to them? It is the person who harms us. By preventing us from gaining a good reputation and other worldly attainments, he helps us to strengthen our desire to attain liberation and enlightenment. By forcing us to practice patience, he is our greatest teacher. He helps us to cut our attachment to reputation and fame and to sever the rope that binds us to samsara. He prevents us from creating the causes to be reborn in this swamp of suffering and instead helps us to create the causes of full enlightenment. By seeing him as our Spiritual Guide who benefits us in so many ways, we should abandon all anger we might feel toward this best friend of ours.

Why should I think of those who harm me as my best friends? When someone harms me, he or she interrupts my Dharma practice, prevents me from accumulating merit and hinders my practice of giving and other virtues. This person is clearly not my friend at such times.

Again, this is wrong. The opportunity to practice patience—one of the most important elements of the spiritual path—arises solely due to the kindness of a person such as this. By giving us a chance to practice patience, this difficult person helps us create extensive merit, yet if we retaliate this opportunity is lost. With no one to test our patience, it will never improve; and without perfecting our patience we can never attain enlightenment. It is therefore a mistake to think that a difficult person can interrupt our Dharma practice. After all, a person in need is not an obstacle to someone who wishes to practice giving, nor an Abbot an obstacle to someone who wishes to take monastic ordination. Far from being obstacles, they are absolute necessities.

We underestimate the value of patience. It is possible that people might sometimes interrupt our meditation sessions or Dharma study, but they can never take away our opportunity to train in inner virtues such as patience. It is this mental training, rather than outer virtuous activities, that is the essence of Dharma practice. If we truly understand the value of patience, we will never resent an opportunity to practice it. Even if we never found the opportunity to sit down to study and meditate throughout our entire life, but we truly learned to practice patient acceptance every moment of the day, we would make vast progress on the path to enlightenment. On the other hand, if we spent our whole life studying and meditating but we never practiced patience, our spiritual practice would remain superficial and inauthentic.

If we truly understand the value of patience, we will never resent an opportunity to practice it.

In general, patience is a stronger virtue than giving because the object of patience is more difficult to find than the object of giving. There are many poor people we can give to, but how many people are trying to harm us and are thereby giving us the opportunity to practice patience? We should think about the rarity of finding such an object of our patience, and recognize our enemy as a source of inexhaustible inner wealth, as well as a true teacher on our path toward the unsurpassable bliss of enlightenment. Instead of seeing the person who tests our patience as an obstacle to our spiritual practice, we should constantly remember his or her kindness and feel joy at having found such a person. It is he who has made our practice of patience possible, and whatever virtue or positive energy arises from this opportunity should be dedicated first to him.

But since my enemy has no intention to help me practice patience, I have no reason to respect him.
If this objection were valid, it would follow that we also have no reason to respect the sacred Dharma, because it too has no intention to help us.

This is not the same thing at all. My enemy harbors harmful thoughts against me, whereas the sacred Dharma does not.
But it is precisely because of the harmful intentions of our enemy that we have the opportunity to practice patience. If, like a doctor who only wishes to benefit his patient, our enemy tried to do us good, we would never have the opportunity to train our mind in non-retaliation. Therefore, even though our enemy has no intention of helping us with our practice, he or she is still worthy to be an object of our veneration, like the sacred Dharma.

Buddha Shakyamuni said that there are two fields for cultivating the crops of virtue: the field of enlightened beings and the field of sentient beings. Through developing faith in the former and striving to benefit the latter, both our own and others' purposes will be fulfilled. These two fields are similar because both yield benefit and both need to be cultivated if we wish to attain enlightenment.

If the two Fields of Merit are equally valuable, why do we make prostrations and offerings to the Buddhas but not to sentient beings?

The point here is not that enlightened beings and ordinary beings share the same qualities—which they clearly do not—but that they are similar in both being causes of our enlightenment, and as such are equally worthy of our respect.

When we give material goods, love, protection or spiritual teachings to living beings, we generally call this "the practice of giving," but when we give to enlightened beings we call this "making offerings." However, because a Bodhisattva regards all sentient beings as infinitely precious and is grateful for the benefit he receives from them, he naturally views his deeds of giving as offerings to them. He recognizes that by acting as the objects of his virtuous actions these beings allow him to reap the fruits of spiritual practice. Thus, along with the Three Jewels, they are also his Field of Merit.

Buddha explained that there is immeasurable merit to be gained from respecting someone who has developed the mind of limitless love. Since such a person has in his heart the welfare of countless beings, any service we do for him indirectly serves all these beings. Just as helping the mother of many children indirectly helps all her children, so any service we do for such a great-hearted being indirectly serves all living beings. Since the mind of limitless love can only be developed in dependence upon its object—limitless living beings—all the merit we create through venerating someone who has the realization of universal love in reality arises due to the kindness of all living beings.

There is also infinite merit created through respecting and developing faith in the Buddhas, because a Buddha's qualities are inconceivably vast and profound. Since being respectful to both Buddhas and sentient beings produces limitless merit and leads to the attainment of full enlightenment, from this point of view Buddhas and sentient beings are equal. However, since sentient beings do not possess infinite good qualities, in this respect they are not equal to the Buddhas.

The qualities of a Buddha are so extensive that any being who shares even a small fraction of them is worthy of great devotion. Even though the vast majority of sentient beings have none of the profound qualities of a Buddha, they are still worthy of our highest respect and devotion because they share in the role of being our Field of Merit. Since living beings are absolutely essential for both our day-to-day happiness and our attainment of full enlightenment, surely it is appropriate to respect them as we would a Buddha?

Due to the kindness of the compassionate Buddhas who reveal the spiritual path, countless living beings have the opportunity to study these teachings and attain enlightenment. How can we repay this infinite kindness? The perfect way of repaying a Buddha, whose sole concern is for the welfare of all living beings, is for us to generate love and compassion for them as well. In his previous lives while following the Bodhisattva path, Buddha Shakyamuni gave up his life many times for the benefit of living beings. How can we harm those for whom Buddha sacrificed his life? Even when they harm us, we should refrain from retaliating and instead try to respond by giving them as much respect, love and help as we can. If we learn to do this, all the Buddhas will be delighted.

We should consider it a privilege to serve sentient beings.

It was out of his infinite love and compassion for all sentient beings that Buddha Shakyamuni gave up everything to seek full enlightenment. Having attained enlightenment, he continues to look upon all sentient beings with boundless love, stronger even than the love of a mother for her dearest child. If all sentient beings are worthy of the love of one such as Buddha, then it goes without saying that ordinary beings like us should also respect them. How can we think of harming those who are the objects of all the Buddhas' love and care? Since the Buddhas with their limitless wisdom, power and good qualities have given their lives completely to the service of sentient beings, we should likewise consider it a privilege to serve sentient beings.

There is no sense in relying upon Buddha yet continuing to harm sentient beings. This is like acting kindly toward a mother but turning and striking her children. Just as we harm a mother by harming her children, so we displease the Buddhas by having negative intentions toward sentient beings. Making offerings to the Buddhas while harming sentient beings is like giving flowers to a mother after torturing her children.

In *Guide to the Bodhisattva's Way of Life* Shantideva summarizes the conclusions we should draw from the above in the following heartfelt prayer:

> Therefore, since I have caused harm to living beings,
> Which has displeased the compassionate Buddhas,
> Today I confess individually all these non-virtues—
> Please, O Compassionate Ones, forgive me for
>   offending you so.
>
> From now on, to delight the Tathagatas,
> I will definitely become like a servant to all living
>   beings.
> Even if people kick me and humiliate me,
> I will please the Buddhas by not retaliating.

One of the most powerful techniques for developing and maintaining bodhichitta is the meditation known as "exchanging self with others." There is no doubt that the Tathagatas—the compassionate Buddhas—have fully accomplished this exchange, and having abandoned all self-cherishing, cherish sentient beings more than themselves. Because all sentient beings are the object of Buddha's cherishing, they are precious. If the Buddhas with their perfect wisdom have seen that sentient beings are worthy of their infinite love and respect, then they are worthy of our respect too.

Anyone who practices the patience of non-retaliation when harmed, and who respects all sentient beings as if they were enlightened beings, pleases all the Buddhas and dispels the misery of the universe by attaining full enlightenment. For this reason, we should always practice patience.

What does it mean to show the same respect to sentient beings as we do to a Buddha? Clearly it would not be appropriate to make full-length prostrations in front of every person we meet. However, we can always respect them mentally, remembering that they are the objects of the Buddhas' love and the cause of our attainment of enlightenment, and we can try to love them and fulfill their wishes. Moreover, all sentient beings have been our mother many times and have shown us untold kindness. All are therefore deserving of our gratitude, love and patience.

If we remember the kindness of all sentient beings and try to please them whenever we can, we will find happiness even in this lifetime. Others will respect us, our fame will spread widely and we will find abundant wealth and possessions. Eventually, as a result of our virtuous actions, we will attain the supreme bliss of Buddhahood. Even if we do not attain Buddhahood in this life, wherever we are reborn in samsara we will reap the benefits of practicing patience. We will have a beautiful body and be surrounded by a circle of devoted friends and students. We will also have good health and a long life.

In conclusion, whenever we experience hardship, disturbances or sickness, we should reflect on the faults of not accepting these and the benefits of being patient with our suffering. Then we should apply the appropriate opponent force by meditating on the patience of voluntarily accepting suffering. To improve and finally perfect our patience, we should meditate on Buddha's teachings on emptiness and the interdependence of all phenomena, and thus practice the patience of definitely thinking about Dharma. Whenever someone harms us, we should remember the many faults of anger and of displeasing sentient beings and overcome these by relying on the patience of not retaliating.

By sincerely practicing these three types of patience, we will extract the greatest possible meaning from our precious human rebirth and waste no more time binding ourself to samsara, the wheel of suffering and dissatisfaction. In these degenerate times, when the causes of suffering abound and it is rare for even a day to pass without our experiencing physical or mental problems, the practice of patience is of supreme importance. Through patiently accepting all difficulties and mistreatment, we will quickly weaken our self-cherishing and self-grasping, thereby allowing the great heart of compassion and bodhichitta to grow. In the midst of this increasingly problematic world, all the qualities of enlightenment will awaken in our mind, and we will truly be able to benefit others.

Dedication

Through the virtues I have accumulated by composing this book, may compassion and wisdom develop and increase for everyone. Through this may all suffering quickly cease, and may we experience permanent world peace and everlasting happiness.

Appendix I

Understanding the Mind

Understanding the Mind

Buddha taught that everything depends upon the mind. To realize this, we must first understand the nature and functions of the mind. At first, this might seem to be quite straightforward since we all have minds and we all know what state our mind is in—whether it is happy or sad, clear or confused and so on. However, if someone were to ask us what the nature of our mind is and how it functions, we would probably not be able to give a precise answer. This indicates that we do not have a clear understanding of the mind.

Some people think that the mind is the brain or some other part or function of the body, but this is incorrect. The brain is a physical object that can be seen with the eyes and that can be photographed or operated on in surgery. The mind, on the other hand, is not a physical object. It cannot be seen with the eyes, nor can it be photographed or repaired by surgery. The brain, therefore, is not the mind but simply part of the body.

There is nothing within the body that can be identified as being our mind because our body and mind are different entities. For example, sometimes when our body is relaxed and immobile, our mind can be very busy, darting from one object to another. This indicates that our body and mind are not the same entity. In the Buddhist scriptures, our body is compared to a guesthouse and our mind to a guest dwelling within it. When we die, our mind leaves our body and goes to the next life, just like a guest leaving a guesthouse and going somewhere else.

If the mind is not the brain, nor any other part of the body, what is it? It is a formless continuum that functions to perceive and understand objects. Because the mind is formless, or non-physical, by nature, it is not obstructed by physical objects. Thus, it is impossible for our body to go to the moon without traveling in a spaceship, but our mind can reach the moon in an instant just by thinking about it. Knowing and perceiving objects is the uncommon function of the mind. Although we say, "I know such and such," in reality it is our mind that knows. We know things only by using our mind.

There are three levels of mind: gross, subtle and very subtle. Gross minds include sense awarenesses such as eye awareness and ear awareness, and all strong delusions such as anger, jealousy, attachment and strong self-grasping ignorance. These gross minds are related to gross inner winds and are relatively easy to recognize. When we fall asleep or die, our gross minds dissolve inward and our subtle minds become manifest. Subtle minds are related to subtle inner winds and are more difficult to recognize than gross minds. During deep sleep, and at the end of the death process, the inner winds dissolve into the center of the heart channel wheel inside the central channel, and then the very subtle mind, the mind of clear light, becomes manifest. The very subtle mind is related to the very subtle inner wind and is extremely difficult to recognize. The continuum of the very subtle mind has no beginning and no end. It is this mind that goes from one life to the next, and if it is completely purified by training in meditation, it is this mind that will eventually transform into the omniscient mind of a Buddha.

It is very important to be able to distinguish unpeaceful states of mind from peaceful states. States of mind that disturb our inner peace, such as anger, jealousy and desirous attachment, are called "delusions." These are the principal causes of all our suffering. We may think that our suffering is caused by other people, by poor material conditions or by society, but in reality it all comes from our own deluded states of mind. The essence of Dharma practice is to reduce and eventually to completely eradicate our delusions, and to replace them with peaceful, virtuous states of mind. This is the main purpose of training in meditation.

Normally we seek happiness outside ourself. We try to obtain better material conditions, a better job, higher social status and so on; but no matter how successful we are in improving our external situation, we still experience many problems and much dissatisfaction. We never experience pure, lasting happiness. In his Dharma teachings, Buddha advises us not to seek happiness outside ourself but to establish it within our mind. How can we do this?

By purifying and controlling our mind through the sincere practice of Buddhadharma. If we train in this way, we can ensure that our mind remains calm and happy all the time. Then, no matter how difficult our external circumstances may be, we will always be happy and peaceful.

Even though we work very hard to find happiness, it remains elusive for us, whereas sufferings and problems seem to come naturally, without any effort. Why is this? It is because the cause of happiness within our mind—virtue—is very weak and can give rise to its effect only if we apply great effort, whereas the internal causes of suffering and problems—the delusions—are very strong and can give rise to their effect with no effort on our part. This is the real reason why problems come naturally while happiness is so difficult to find.

From this we can see that the principal causes of both happiness and problems are in the mind, not in the external world. If we were able to maintain a calm and peaceful mind all day long, we would never experience any problems or mental suffering. For example, if our mind remains peaceful all the time, then even if we are insulted, criticized or blamed, or if we lose our job or our friends, we will not become unhappy. No matter how difficult our external circumstances may become, for as long as we maintain a calm and peaceful mind, the situation will not be a problem for us. Therefore, if we wish to be free from problems there is only one thing to do—learn to maintain a peaceful state of mind by practicing Dharma sincerely and purely.

Appendix II

Past and Future Lives

Past and Future Lives

If we understand the nature of the mind, we can also understand the existence of past and future lives. Many people believe that when the body disintegrates at death, the continuum of the mind ceases and the mind becomes non-existent, like a candle flame going out when all the wax has burned. There are even some people who contemplate committing suicide in the hope that if they die their problems and sufferings will come to an end. However, these ideas are completely wrong. As explained in Appendix I, our body and mind are separate entities, and so even though the body disintegrates at death, the continuum of the mind remains unbroken. Instead of ceasing, the mind simply leaves the present body and goes to the next life. For ordinary beings, therefore, rather than releasing us from suffering, death only brings new sufferings. Not understanding this, many people destroy their precious human life by committing suicide.

One way to gain an understanding of past and future lives is to examine the process of sleeping, dreaming and waking, because this closely resembles the process of death, intermediate state and rebirth. When we fall asleep, our gross inner winds gather and dissolve inward, and our mind becomes progressively more and more subtle until it transforms into the very subtle mind of the clear light of sleep. While the clear light of sleep is manifest, we experience deep sleep, and to others we resemble a dead person. When the clear light of sleep ends, our mind becomes gradually more and more gross and we pass through the various levels of the dream state. Finally, our normal powers of memory and mental control are restored and we wake up. When this happens our dream world disappears and we perceive the world of the waking state.

A very similar process occurs when we die. As we die, our winds dissolve inward and our mind becomes progressively more and more subtle until the very subtle mind of the clear light of death becomes manifest. The experience of the clear light of death is very similar to the experience of deep sleep. After the clear light of death has ceased, we experience the stages of the intermediate state, or "bardo" in Tibetan, which is a dream-like state that occurs between death and rebirth. After a few days or weeks, the intermediate state ends and we take rebirth. Just as when we wake from sleep, the dream world disappears and we perceive the world of the waking state, so when we take rebirth, the appearances of the intermediate state cease and we perceive the world of our next life.

The only significant difference between the process of sleeping, dreaming and waking and the process of death, intermediate state and rebirth is that after the clear light of sleep has ceased, the relationship between our mind and our present body remains intact, whereas after the clear light of death this relationship is broken. By contemplating this, we will gain conviction in the existence of past and future lives.

We generally believe that the things we perceive in dreams are unreal whereas the things we perceive when we are awake are true; but Buddha said that all phenomena are like dreams in that they are mere appearances to mind. For those who can interpret them correctly, dreams have great significance. For example, if we dream that we visit a particular country to which we have not been in this life, our dream will indicate one of four things: that we have been to that country in a previous life, that we will visit it later in this life, that we will visit it in a future life or that it has some personal significance for us, as it would, for example, if we had recently received a letter from that country or had seen a television program about it. Similarly, if we dream we are flying, it may mean that in a previous life we were a being who could fly, such as a bird or a meditator with miracle powers, or it may predict that we will become such a being in the future. A flying dream may also have a less literal meaning, symbolizing an improvement in our health or state of mind.

It was with the help of dreams that I was able to discover where my mother was reborn after she had died. Just before she died, my mother dozed off for a few minutes and when she woke she told my sister, who was caring for her, that she had dreamed of me and that in her dream I had offered her a traditional white scarf, or khatag. I took this dream to mean that I would be able to help my mother in her next life, and so after she died, I prayed every day for her to be reborn in England, where I was living, so that I would have the opportunity to meet and recognize her reincarnation. I made strong requests to my Dharmapala to show me clear signs of where my mother's reincarnation could be found.

Later, I had three dreams that seemed to be significant. In the first, I dreamed that I met my mother in a place I took to be England. I asked her how she had traveled from India to England, but she replied that she had not come from India but from Switzerland. In the second dream, I saw my mother talking to a group of people. I approached her and spoke to her in Tibetan, but she did not seem to understand what I was saying. While she was alive, my mother spoke only Tibetan, but in this dream she spoke English fluently. I asked her why she had forgotten Tibetan, but she did not reply. Later in the same dream, I dreamed of a Western couple who are helping with the development of Dharma Centers in Britain.

Both dreams seemed to give clues as to where my mother had been reborn. Two days after the second dream, the husband of the couple of whom I had dreamed visited me and told me that his wife was pregnant. I immediately remembered my dream and thought that her baby might be my mother's reincarnation. The fact that in the dream my mother had forgotten Tibetan and spoke only English suggested that she would be reborn in an English-speaking country, and the presence of this couple in the dream might have been an indication that they were her parents. I then performed a traditional divination together with ritual prayers, called a *mo* in Tibetan, and this indicated that their child was my mother's reincarnation. I was very happy but did not say anything to anyone.

One night I dreamed about my mother again and again. The next morning, I considered the matter carefully and reached a decision. If the baby had been born that night, then it was definitely my mother's reincarnation, but if it had not, I would need to make further examinations. Having made this decision, I phoned the husband, who gave me the good news that his wife had given birth to a baby girl the previous night. I was delighted and performed a puja, or offering ceremony, as a thanksgiving to my Dharmapala.

A few days later, the father phoned and told me that if he recited the mantra of Buddha Avalokiteshvara, OM MANI PÄME HUM, when the baby cried, she would immediately stop crying and appear to be listening to the mantra. He asked me why this was and I replied that it was because of her tendencies from her previous life. I knew that my mother had recited this mantra with strong faith throughout her life.

The child was named Amaravajra. Later, when my mother's brother, Kuten Lama, visited England and saw Amaravajra for the first time, he was astonished by how affectionate she was toward him. He said that it was as if she recognized him. I also had the same experience. Although I was able to visit the young child only very occasionally, she was always extremely happy to see me.

When Amaravajra started to talk, one day she pointed to a dog and said, "kyi, kyi." After this, she used to say "kyi" many times whenever she saw a dog. Her father asked me if "kyi" meant anything, and I told him that in the dialect of western Tibet, where my mother lived, "kyi" means "dog." This was not the only Tibetan word the little girl uttered spontaneously.

I later heard through my sister's husband that after my mother's death, a Tibetan astrologer had predicted that my mother would be born as a female in a country with a language other than Tibetan. This story comes from my own personal experience, but if we investigate we can find many other true stories about how people have been able to recognize the reincarnations of their Teachers, parents, friends and others. If we contemplate such stories, and reflect on the nature of the mind and the experience of dreams, we will definitely become convinced of the existence of past and future lives.

In his Tantric teachings, Buddha taught a special practice called "transference of consciousness into another body." This practice became quite widespread in the early days of Buddhism in Tibet. One practitioner who mastered it was Tarma Dode, the son of the famous Tibetan lay Lama and translator, Marpa. One day, while riding a horse, Tarma Dode fell and fatally injured his body. Knowing that his son had mastered the practice of transference of consciousness, Marpa immediately began searching for a corpse into which Tarma Dode could transfer his consciousness. Unable to find a human corpse, Marpa brought his son a pigeon's corpse, which would serve as a temporary abode for his mind until he could find a suitable human corpse. Tarma Dode then ejected his mind from his dying human body and entered into the corpse of the pigeon. Immediately, Tarma Dode's old human body died and the pigeon's body came back to life. Tarma Dode's body was now the body of a pigeon, but his mind was still the mind of a human being.

Since he did not want his son to remain in the form of a pigeon, Marpa continued to search for a qualified human corpse. One day, with his clairvoyance, he saw that a Buddhist Teacher had just died in India and that his disciples had taken his corpse to the cemetery. Marpa told his son to fly to India as quickly as possible. Tarma Dode then flew to India in his pigeon's body, and when he arrived at the place where the Teacher's corpse had been left, he ejected his mind from the pigeon's body and entered the corpse. The body of the pigeon immediately died and the body of the deceased Teacher came back to life. Tarma Dode then spent the remainder of his life as an Indian Teacher known as Tiwu Sangnak Dongpo. Some years later, Marpa's principal disciple, Milarepa, sent his own disciple, Rechungpa, to India to receive special teachings from Tiwu Sangnak Dongpo. When Rechungpa returned to Tibet, he offered these instructions to Milarepa.

There are many other examples of past meditators who could transfer their consciousness into other bodies. It is said that Marpa himself practiced transference of consciousness into another body four times during his life. If mind and body were the same entity, how would it be possible for these meditators to transfer their consciousness in this way? If we contemplate true stories such as these with a positive mind, it will help us understand how it is possible for consciousness to continue beyond the death of the body. This in turn will make it very easy for us to understand the existence of past and future lives.

Appendix III

Liberating Prayer

PRAISE TO BUDDHA SHAKYAMUNI

and

Prayers for Meditation

BRIEF PREPARATORY PRAYERS
FOR MEDITATION

Be victorious over the enemy of your delusions

Liberating Prayer

PRAISE TO BUDDHA SHAKYAMUNI

O Blessed One, Shakyamuni Buddha,
Precious treasury of compassion,
Bestower of supreme inner peace,

You, who love all beings without exception,
Are the source of happiness and goodness;
And you guide us to the liberating path.

Your body is a wishfulfilling jewel,
Your speech is supreme, purifying nectar,
And your mind is refuge for all living beings.

With folded hands I turn to you,
Supreme unchanging friend,
I request from the depths of my heart:

Please give me the light of your wisdom
To dispel the darkness of my mind
And to heal my mental continuum.

Please nourish me with your goodness,
That I in turn may nourish all beings
With an unceasing banquet of delight.

Through your compassionate intention,
Your blessings and virtuous deeds,
And my strong wish to rely upon you,

May all suffering quickly cease
And all happiness and joy be fulfilled;
And may holy Dharma flourish for evermore.

Colophon: This prayer was composed by Venerable Geshe Kelsang Gyatso Rinpoche and is recited regularly at the beginning of teachings, meditations and prayers in Kadampa Buddhist Centers throughout the world.

Prayers for Meditation

BRIEF PREPARATORY PRAYERS FOR MEDITATION

Going for refuge

I and all sentient beings, until we achieve enlightenment,
Go for refuge to Buddha, Dharma and Sangha.

(3x, 7x, 100x or more)

Generating bodhichitta

Through the virtues I collect by giving and other
    perfections,
May I become a Buddha for the benefit of all.   (3x)

Generating the four immeasurables

May everyone be happy,
May everyone be free from misery,
May no one ever be separated from their happiness,
May everyone have equanimity, free from hatred and
    attachment.

Visualizing the Field for Accumulating Merit

In the space before me is the living Buddha Shakyamuni surrounded by all the Buddhas and Bodhisattvas, like the full moon surrounded by stars.

Prayer of seven limbs

With my body, speech and mind, humbly I prostrate,
And make offerings both set out and imagined.
I confess my wrong deeds from all time,
And rejoice in the virtues of all.
Please stay until samsara ceases,
And turn the Wheel of Dharma for us.
I dedicate all virtues to great enlightenment.

Offering the mandala

The ground sprinkled with perfume and spread with
   flowers,
The Great Mountain, four lands, sun and moon,
Seen as a Buddha Land and offered thus,
May all beings enjoy such Pure Lands.

I offer without any sense of loss
The objects that give rise to my attachment, hatred and
   confusion,
My friends, enemies and strangers, our bodies and
   enjoyments;
Please accept these and bless me to be released directly
   from the three poisons.

IDAM GURU RATNA MANDALAKAM NIRYATAYAMI

Prayer of the Stages of the Path

The path begins with strong reliance
On my kind Teacher, source of all good;
O Bless me with this understanding
To follow him with great devotion.

This human life with all its freedoms,
Extremely rare, with so much meaning;
O Bless me with this understanding
All day and night to seize its essence.

My body, like a water bubble,
Decays and dies so very quickly;
After death come results of karma,
Just like the shadow of a body.

With this firm knowledge and remembrance
Bless me to be extremely cautious,
Always avoiding harmful actions
And gathering abundant virtue.

Samsara's pleasures are deceptive,
Give no contentment, only torment;
So please bless me to strive sincerely
To gain the bliss of perfect freedom.

O Bless me so that from this pure thought
Come mindfulness and greatest caution,
To keep as my essential practice
The doctrine's root, the Pratimoksha.

Just like myself all my kind mothers
Are drowning in samsara's ocean;
O So that I may soon release them,
Bless me to train in bodhichitta.

But I cannot become a Buddha
By this alone without three ethics;
So bless me with the strength to practice
The Bodhisattva's ordination.

By pacifying my distractions
And analyzing perfect meanings,
Bless me to quickly gain the union
Of special insight and quiescence.

When I become a pure container
Through common paths, bless me to enter
The essence practice of good fortune,
The supreme vehicle, Vajrayana.

The two attainments both depend on
My sacred vows and my commitments;
Bless me to understand this clearly
And keep them at the cost of my life.

By constant practice in four sessions,
The way explained by holy Teachers,
O Bless me to gain both the stages,
Which are the essence of the Tantras.

May those who guide me on the good path,
And my companions all have long lives;
Bless me to pacify completely
All obstacles, outer and inner.

May I always find perfect Teachers,
And take delight in holy Dharma,
Accomplish all grounds and paths swiftly,
And gain the state of Vajradhara.

Receiving blessings and purifying

From the hearts of all the holy beings, streams of light
and nectar flow down, granting blessings and purifying.

*At this point we begin the actual contemplation and
meditation. After the meditation we dedicate our merit
while reciting the following prayers:*

Dedication prayers

Through the virtues I have collected
By practicing the stages of the path,
May all living beings find the opportunity
To practice in the same way.

May everyone experience
The happiness of humans and gods,
And quickly attain enlightenment,
So that samsara is finally extinguished.

Prayers for the Virtuous Tradition

So that the tradition of Je Tsongkhapa,
The King of the Dharma, may flourish,
May all obstacles be pacified
And may all favorable conditions abound.

Through the two collections of myself and others
Gathered throughout the three times,
May the doctrine of Conqueror Losang Dragpa
Flourish for evermore.

The nine-line *Migtsema* prayer

Tsongkhapa, crown ornament of the scholars
    of the Land of the Snows,
You are Buddha Shakyamuni and Vajradhara,
    the source of all attainments,
Avalokiteshvara, the treasury of unobservable
    compassion,
Manjushri, the supreme stainless wisdom,
And Vajrapani, the destroyer of the hosts of maras.
O Venerable Guru-Buddha, synthesis of all
    Three Jewels,
With my body, speech and mind, respectfully I
    make requests:
Please grant your blessings to ripen and
    liberate myself and others,
And bestow the common and supreme attainments. (3x)

Colophon: This sadhana, or ritual prayer for spiritual attainments, was compiled from traditional sources by Venerable Geshe Kelsang Gyatso Rinpoche.

Appendix IV

What is Meditation?

What is Meditation?

Meditation is a mind that concentrates on a virtuous object, and a mental action that is the main cause of mental peace. Whenever we meditate, we are performing an action that will cause us to experience inner peace in the future. Normally, throughout our life, we experience delusions day and night, and these are the opposite to mental peace. Sometimes, however, we naturally experience inner peace, and this is because in our previous lives we concentrated on virtuous objects. A virtuous object is one that causes us to develop a peaceful mind when we concentrate on it. If we concentrate on an object that causes us to develop an unpeaceful mind, such as anger or attachment, this indicates that for us the object is non-virtuous. There are also many neutral objects that are neither virtuous nor non-virtuous.

There are two types of meditation: analytical meditation and placement meditation. Analytical meditation involves contemplating the meaning of a spiritual instruction that we have heard or read. By contemplating such instructions deeply, eventually we will reach a definite conclusion, or cause a specific virtuous state of mind to arise. This is the object of placement meditation. We then concentrate single-pointedly on this conclusion or virtuous state of mind for as long as possible to become deeply acquainted with it. This single-pointed concentration is placement meditation. Analytical meditation is often called "contemplation," and placement meditation is often called "meditation." Placement meditation depends upon analytical meditation, and analytical meditation depends upon listening to or reading spiritual instructions.

THE BENEFITS OF MEDITATION

The purpose of meditation is to make our mind calm and peaceful. As mentioned in Appendix I, if our mind is peaceful we will be free from worries and mental discomfort, and so we will experience true happiness; but if our mind is not peaceful, we will find it very difficult to be happy, even if we are living in the very best conditions. If we train in meditation, our mind will gradually become more and more peaceful, and we will experience a purer and purer form of happiness. Eventually, we will be able to stay happy all the time, even in the most difficult circumstances.

Usually we find it difficult to control our mind. It seems as if our mind is like a balloon in the wind—blown here and there by external circumstances. If things go well our mind is happy, but if they go badly it immediately becomes unhappy. For example, if we get what we want, such as a new possession, a new position or a new partner, we become overly excited and cling to them tightly; but since we cannot have everything we want, and since we will inevitably be separated from the friends, position and possessions we currently enjoy, this mental stickiness, or attachment, serves only to cause us pain. On the other hand, if we do not get what we want, or if we lose something that we like, we become despondent or irritated. For example, if we are forced to work with a colleague whom we dislike, we will probably become irritated and feel aggrieved, with the result that we will be unable to work with him or her efficiently and our time at work will become stressful and unrewarding.

Such fluctuations of mood arise because we are too closely involved in the external situation. We are like a child making a sandcastle who is excited when it is first made, but who becomes upset when it is destroyed by the incoming tide. By training in meditation, we create an inner space and clarity that enables us to control our mind regardless of the external circumstances. Gradually we develop mental equilibrium, a balanced mind that is happy all the time, rather than an unbalanced mind that oscillates between the extremes of excitement and despondency.

If we train in meditation systematically, eventually we will be able to eradicate from our mind the delusions that are the causes of all our problems and suffering. In this way, we will come to experience permanent inner peace. Then day and night, in life after life, we will experience only peace and happiness.

At the beginning, even if our meditation does not seem to be going well, we should remember that simply by applying effort to training in meditation, we are creating the mental karma to experience inner peace in the future. The happiness of this life and of our future lives depends upon the experience of inner peace, which in turn depends upon the mental action of meditation. Since inner peace is the source of all happiness, we can see how important meditation is.

HOW TO BEGIN MEDITATION

The first stage of meditation is to stop distractions and make our mind clearer and more lucid. This can be accomplished by practicing a simple breathing meditation. We choose a quiet place to meditate and sit in a comfortable position. We can sit in the traditional cross-legged posture or in any other position that is comfortable. If we wish, we can sit in a chair. The most important thing is to keep our back straight to prevent our mind from becoming sluggish or sleepy.

We sit with our eyes partially closed and turn our attention to our breathing. We breathe naturally, preferably through the nostrils, without attempting to control our breath, and we try to become aware of the sensation of the breath as it enters and leaves the nostrils. This sensation is our object of meditation. We should try to concentrate on it to the exclusion of everything else.

At first our mind will be very busy, and we might even feel that the meditation is making our mind busier; but in reality we are just becoming more aware of how busy our mind actually is. There will be a great temptation to follow the different thoughts as they arise, but we should resist this and remain focused single-pointedly on the sensation of the breath. If we discover that our mind has wandered and is following our thoughts, we should immediately return it to the breath. We should repeat this as many times as necessary until the mind settles on the breath.

If we practice patiently in this way, gradually our distracting thoughts will subside and we will experience a sense of inner peace and relaxation. Our mind will feel lucid and spacious and we will feel refreshed. When the sea is rough, sediment is churned up and the water becomes murky, but when the wind dies down the mud gradually settles and the water becomes clear. In a similar way, when the otherwise incessant flow of our distracting thoughts is calmed through concentrating on the breath, our mind becomes unusually lucid and clear. We should stay with this state of mental calm for a while.

Even though breathing meditation is only a preliminary stage of meditation, it can be quite powerful. We can see from this practice that it is possible to experience inner peace and contentment just by controlling the mind, without having to depend at all on external conditions. When the turbulence of distracting thoughts subsides and our mind becomes still, a deep happiness and contentment naturally arises from within. This feeling of contentment and well-being helps us cope with the busyness and difficulties of daily life. So much of the stress and tension we normally experience comes from our mind, and many of the problems we experience, including poor health, are caused or aggravated by this stress. Just by doing breathing meditation for ten or fifteen minutes each day, we will be able to reduce this stress. We will experience a calm, spacious feeling in the mind and many of our usual problems will fall away. Difficult situations will become easier to deal with, we will naturally feel warm and well-disposed toward other people and our relationships with others will gradually improve.

We should train in this preliminary meditation until we reduce our gross distractions, and then we can train in the actual meditations such as those explained in *The New Meditation Handbook*. When we do these meditations, we should begin by calming the mind with breathing meditation, and then proceed to the stages of analytical and placement meditation according to the specific instructions for each meditation.

Appendix V

The Kadampa Way of Life

THE ESSENTIAL PRACTICE
OF KADAM LAMRIM

Benefit others by turning the Wheel of Dharma

Introduction

This essential practice of Kadam Lamrim, known as *The Kadampa Way of Life*, contains two texts: *Advice from Atisha's Heart* and Je Tsongkhapa's *The Three Principal Aspects of the Path*. The first encapsulates the way of life of the early Kadampa practitioners, whose example of purity and sincerity we should all try to emulate. The second is a profound guide to meditation on the stages of the path, Lamrim, which Je Tsongkhapa composed based on the instructions he received directly from the Wisdom Buddha Manjushri.

If we try our best to put Atisha's advice into practice, and to meditate on Lamrim according to Je Tsongkhapa's instructions, we will develop a pure and happy mind and gradually progress toward the ultimate peace of full enlightenment. As Bodhisattva Shantideva says:

By depending upon this boat-like human form,
We can cross the great ocean of suffering.
Since such a vessel will be hard to find again,
This is no time to sleep, you fool!

Practicing in this way is the very essence of the Kadampa way of life.

Advice from Atisha's Heart

When Venerable Atisha came to Tibet, he first went to Ngari, where he remained for two years giving many teachings to the disciples of Jangchub Ö. After two years had passed, he decided to return to India, and Jangchub Ö requested him to give one last teaching before he left. Atisha replied that he had already given them all the advice they needed, but Jangchub Ö persisted in his request and so Atisha accepted and gave the following advice.

How wonderful!

Friends, since you already have great knowledge and clear understanding, whereas I am of no importance and have little wisdom, it is not suitable for you to request advice from me. However because you dear friends, whom I cherish from my heart, have requested me, I shall give you this essential advice from my inferior and childish mind.

Friends, until you attain enlightenment the Spiritual Teacher is indispensable, therefore rely upon the holy Spiritual Guide.

Until you realize ultimate truth, listening is indispensable, therefore listen to the instructions of the Spiritual Guide.

Since you cannot become a Buddha merely by understanding Dharma, practice earnestly with understanding.

Avoid places that disturb your mind, and always remain where your virtues increase.

Until you attain stable realizations, worldly amusements are harmful, therefore abide in a place where there are no such distractions.

Avoid friends who cause you to increase delusions, and rely upon those who increase your virtue. This you should take to heart.

Since there is never a time when worldly activities come to an end, limit your activities.

Dedicate your virtues throughout the day and the night, and always watch your mind.

Because you have received advice, whenever you are not meditating, always practice in accordance with what your Spiritual Guide says.

If you practice with great devotion, results will arise immediately, without your having to wait for a long time.

If from your heart you practice in accordance with Dharma, both food and resources will come naturally to hand.

Friends, the things you desire give no more satisfaction than drinking sea water, therefore practice contentment.

Avoid all haughty, conceited, proud, and arrogant minds, and remain peaceful and subdued.

Avoid activities that are said to be meritorious, but which in fact are obstacles to Dharma.

Profit and respect are nooses of the maras, so brush them aside like stones on the path.

Words of praise and fame serve only to beguile us, therefore blow them away as you would blow your nose.

Since the happiness, pleasure, and friends you gather in this life last only for a moment, put them all behind you.

Since future lives last for a very long time, gather up riches to provide for the future.

You will have to depart leaving everything behind, so do not be attached to anything.

Generate compassion for lowly beings, and especially avoid despising or humiliating them.

Have no hatred for enemies, and no attachment for friends.

Do not be jealous of others' good qualities, but out of admiration adopt them yourself.

Do not look for faults in others, but look for faults in yourself, and purge them like bad blood.

Do not contemplate your own good qualities, but contemplate the good qualities of others, and respect everyone as a servant would.

See all living beings as your father or mother, and love them as if you were their child.

Always keep a smiling face and a loving mind, and speak truthfully without malice.

If you talk too much with little meaning, you will make mistakes, therefore speak in moderation, only when necessary.

If you engage in many meaningless activities, your virtuous activities will degenerate, therefore stop activities that are not spiritual.

It is completely meaningless to put effort into activities that have no essence.

If the things you desire do not come, it is due to karma created long ago, therefore keep a happy and relaxed mind.

Beware, offending a holy being is worse than dying, therefore be honest and straightforward.

Since all the happiness and suffering of this life arise from previous actions, do not blame others.

All happiness comes from the blessings of your Spiritual Guide, therefore always repay his kindness.

Since you cannot tame the minds of others until you have tamed your own, begin by taming your own mind.

Since you will definitely have to depart without the wealth you have accumulated, do not accumulate negativity for the sake of wealth.

Distracting enjoyments have no essence, therefore sincerely practice giving.

Always keep pure moral discipline for it leads to beauty in this life and happiness hereafter.

Since hatred is rife in these impure times, don the armor of patience, free from anger.

You remain in samsara through the power of laziness, therefore ignite the fire of the effort of application.

Since this human life is wasted by indulging in distractions, now is the time to practice concentration.

Being under the influence of wrong views, you do not realize the ultimate nature of things, therefore investigate correct meanings.

Friends, there is no happiness in this swamp of samsara, so move to the firm ground of liberation.

Meditate according to the advice of your Spiritual Guide and dry up the river of samsaric suffering.

You should consider this well because it is not just words from the mouth, but sincere advice from the heart.

If you practice like this, you will delight me, and you will bring happiness to yourself and others.

I who am ignorant request you to take this advice to heart.

This is the advice that the holy being Venerable Atisha gave to Venerable Jangchub Ö.

The Three Principal Aspects of the Path

Homage to the venerable Spiritual Guide.

I shall explain to the best of my ability
The essential meaning of all the Conqueror's teachings,
The path praised by the holy Bodhisattvas,
And the gateway for fortunate ones seeking liberation.

You who are not attached to the joys of samsara,
But strive to make your freedom and endowment
    meaningful,
O Fortunate Ones who apply your minds to the path
    that pleases the Conquerors,
Please listen with a clear mind.

Without pure renunciation, there is no way to pacify
Attachment to the pleasures of samsara;
And since living beings are tightly bound by desire for
    samsara,
Begin by seeking renunciation.

Freedom and endowment are difficult to find, and there
    is no time to waste.
By acquainting your mind with this, overcome
    attachment to this life;
And by repeatedly contemplating actions and effects
And the sufferings of samsara, overcome attachment to
    future lives.

When, through contemplating in this way, the desire for
    the pleasures of samsara
Does not arise, even for a moment,
But a mind longing for liberation arises throughout the
    day and the night,
At that time, renunciation is generated.

However, if this renunciation is not maintained
By completely pure bodhichitta,
It will not be a cause of the perfect happiness of
    unsurpassed enlightenment;
Therefore, the wise generate a supreme bodhichitta.

Swept along by the currents of the four powerful rivers,
Tightly bound by the chains of karma, so hard to release,
Ensnared within the iron net of self-grasping,
Completely enveloped by the pitch-black darkness of
    ignorance,

Taking rebirth after rebirth in boundless samsara,
And unceasingly tormented by the three sufferings—

Through contemplating the state of your mothers in
  conditions such as these,
Generate a supreme mind [of bodhichitta].

But, even though you may be acquainted with
  renunciation and bodhichitta,
If you do not possess the wisdom realizing the way things
  are,
You will not be able to cut the root of samsara;
Therefore, strive in the means for realizing dependent
  relationship.

Whoever negates the conceived object of self-grasping
Yet sees the infallibility of cause and effect
Of all phenomena in samsara and nirvana,
Has entered the path that pleases the Buddhas.

Dependent-related appearance is infallible
And emptiness is inexpressible;
For as long as the meaning of these two appear to be
  separate,
You have not yet realized Buddha's intention.

When they arise as one, not alternating but
  simultaneous,
From merely seeing infallible dependent relationship
Comes certain knowledge that destroys all grasping at
  objects.
At that time, the analysis of view is complete.

Moreover, when the extreme of existence is dispelled by
  appearance,
And the extreme of non-existence is dispelled by
  emptiness,
And you know how emptiness is perceived as cause and
  effect,
You will not be captivated by extreme views.

When, in this way, you have correctly realized the
  essential points
Of the three principal aspects of the path,
Dear One, withdraw into solitude, generate strong effort,
And quickly accomplish the final goal.

Colophon: Both texts were translated under the compassionate
guidance of Venerable Geshe Kelsang Gyatso Rinpoche.

Glossary

Alertness A mental factor which is a type of wisdom that examines our activity of body, speech and mind and knows whether or not faults are developing. See *How to Understand the Mind*.

Atisha (AD 982–1054) A famous Indian Buddhist scholar and meditation master. He was Abbot of the great Buddhist monastery of Vikramashila at a time when Mahayana Buddhism was flourishing in India. He was later invited to Tibet and his arrival there led to the re-establishment of Buddhism in Tibet. He is the author of the first text on the stages of the path, *Lamp for the Path*. His tradition later became known as the "Kadampa Tradition." See *Modern Buddhism* and *Joyful Path of Good Fortune*.

Attachment A deluded mental factor that observes its contaminated object, regards it as a cause of happiness and wishes for it. See *Joyful Path of Good Fortune* and *How to Understand the Mind*.

Avalokiteshvara The embodiment of the compassion of all the Buddhas. Sometimes he appears with one face and four arms and sometimes with eleven faces and a thousand arms. Called "Chenrezig" in Tibetan. See *Living Meaningfully, Dying Joyfully*.

Beginningless time According to the Buddhist world view, there is no beginning to mind, and so no beginning to time.

Therefore, all sentient beings have taken countless previous rebirths.

Blessing The transformation of our mind from a negative state to a positive state, from an unhappy state to a happy state, or from a state of weakness to a state of strength, through the inspiration of holy beings such as our Spiritual Guide, Buddhas and Bodhisattvas.

Bodhichitta A Sanskrit word for "mind of enlightenment." "Bodhi" means "enlightenment," and "chitta" means "mind." There are two types of bodhichitta—conventional bodhichitta and ultimate bodhichitta. Generally speaking, the term "bodhichitta" refers to conventional bodhichitta, which is a primary mind motivated by great compassion that spontaneously seeks enlightenment to benefit all living beings. There are two types of conventional bodhichitta—aspiring bodhichitta and engaging bodhichitta. Ultimate bodhichitta is a wisdom motivated by conventional bodhichitta that directly realizes emptiness, the ultimate nature of phenomena. See *Joyful Path of Good Fortune, Modern Buddhism, Eight Steps to Happiness* and *Meaningful to Behold*.

Bodhisattva A person who has generated spontaneous bodhichitta but who has not yet become a Buddha. See *Joyful Path of Good Fortune* and *Meaningful to Behold*.

Buddha In general, *"Buddha"* means "Awakened One," someone who has awakened from the sleep of ignorance and sees things as they really are. A Buddha is a person who is completely free from all faults and mental obstructions. Every living being has the potential to become a Buddha. See also **Buddha Shakyamuni.** See *Modern Buddhism* and *Joyful Path of Good Fortune*.

Buddhahood Synonymous with full enlightenment.

Buddha Shakyamuni The Buddha who is the founder of the Buddhist religion. See *Introduction to Buddhism.*

Buddhist Anyone who from the depths of his or her heart goes for refuge to the Three Jewels—Buddha Jewel, Dharma Jewel and Sangha Jewel. See *Introduction to Buddhism.*

Central channel The principal channel at the very center of the body, along which the channel wheels are located. See *Modern Buddhism, Clear Light of Bliss, Tantric Grounds and Paths* and *Mahamudra Tantra.*

Channel wheel "Chakra" in Sanskrit. A focal center where secondary channels branch out from the central channel. Meditating on these points can cause the inner winds to enter the central channel. See *Modern Buddhism, Mahamudra Tantra* and *Tantric Grounds and Paths.*

Chekhawa, Geshe (AD 1102–1176) A great Kadampa Bodhisattva who composed the text *Training the Mind in Seven Points,* a commentary to Geshe Langri Tangpa's *Eight Verses of Training the Mind.* He spread the study and practice of training the mind throughout Tibet. See *Universal Compassion.*

Clear light A manifest very subtle mind that perceives an appearance like clear, empty space. See *Modern Buddhism, Clear Light of Bliss* and *Tantric Grounds and Paths.*

Compassion A virtuous mind that wishes others to be free from suffering. See *Modern Buddhism* and *Eight Steps to Happiness.*

Conqueror A Buddha is called a "Conqueror" because he or she has conquered all four types of mara. See also **Mara.**

Contaminated phenomenon Any phenomenon that gives rise to delusions or that causes them to increase. Examples are the environments, beings and enjoyments of samsara. See *Joyful Path of Good Fortune*.

Contentment Being satisfied with one's inner and outer conditions, motivated by a virtuous intention.

Dedication Dedication is by nature a virtuous intention that functions both to prevent accumulated virtue from degenerating and to cause its increase. See *Joyful Path of Good Fortune*.

Degenerate times A period when spiritual activity degenerates.

Delusion A mental factor that arises from inappropriate attention and functions to make the mind unpeaceful and uncontrolled. There are three main delusions: ignorance, desirous attachment and anger. From these all the other delusions arise, such as jealousy, pride and deluded doubt. See *How to Understand the Mind*.

Dependent relationship A dependent-related phenomenon is any phenomenon that exists in dependence upon other phenomena. All phenomena are dependent related because all phenomena depend on their parts. Sometimes "dependent related" (Tib. *ten drel*) is distinguished from "dependent arising" (Tib. *ten jung*), with the latter meaning arising in dependence upon causes and conditions. However, the two terms are often used interchangeably. See *The New Heart of Wisdom* and *Joyful Path of Good Fortune*.

Dharmapala Sanskrit word for "Dharma Protector," a manifestation of a Buddha or Bodhisattva whose main function is to eliminate obstacles and gather all necessary conditions for pure Dharma practitioners. See *Heart Jewel*.

Emptiness Lack of inherent existence, the ultimate nature of phenomena. See *Modern Buddhism*, *Transform Your Life* and *The New Heart of Wisdom*.

Enlightenment Omniscient wisdom free from all mistaken appearances. See *Modern Buddhism*, *Transform Your Life* and *Joyful Path of Good Fortune*.

Extremes of existence and non-existence Buddha explains the middle way by refuting the two extremes: the extreme of existence (that phenomena are inherently existent), and the extreme of non-existence (that phenomena do not exist at all).

Extreme view A deluded view that observes the I that is the conceived object of the view of the transitory collection and grasps it either as permanent or as completely ceasing at the time of death. See *How to Understand the Mind*.

Faith A naturally virtuous mind that functions mainly to oppose the perception of faults in its observed object. There are three types of faith: believing faith, admiring faith and wishing faith. See *Modern Buddhism*, *Transform Your Life* and *How to Understand the Mind*.

Feeling A mental factor that functions to experience pleasant, unpleasant or neutral objects. See *How to Understand the Mind*.

Geshe A title given by Kadampa monasteries to accomplished Buddhist scholars. A contracted form of the Tibetan "ge wai she nyen," literally meaning "virtuous friend."

"Guide to the Bodhisattva's Way of Life" A classic Mahayana Buddhist text composed by the great Indian Buddhist Yogi and scholar Shantideva, which presents all the practices of a Bodhisattva from the initial generation of bodhichitta through to the completion of the practice of the six perfections. For a translation, see *Guide to the Bodhisattva's Way of Life*. For a full commentary, see *Meaningful to Behold*.

Hell realm The lowest of the six realms of samsara. See *Joyful Path of Good Fortune*.

Imprint There are two types of imprint: imprints of actions and imprints of delusions. Every action we perform leaves an imprint on the mental consciousness, and these imprints are karmic potentialities to experience certain effects in the future. The imprints left by delusions remain even after the delusions themselves have been abandoned, like the smell of garlic lingers in a container after the garlic has been removed. Imprints of delusions are obstructions to omniscience and are completely abandoned only by Buddhas.

Imputation According to the Madhyamika-Prasangika school, all phenomena are merely imputed by conception in dependence upon their basis of imputation. Therefore, they are mere imputation and do not exist from their own side at all. See *Modern Buddhism* and *The New Heart of Wisdom*.

Inherent existence An imagined mode of existence whereby phenomena are held to exist from their own side, independent of other phenomena. In reality all phenomena lack, or are empty of, inherent existence because they depend on their parts. See *Modern Buddhism* and *The New Heart of Wisdom*.

Inner winds Special subtle winds related to the mind that flow through the channels of our body. Our body and mind cannot function without these winds. See *Modern Buddhism*, *Mahamudra Tantra*, *Clear Light of Bliss* and *Tantric Grounds and Paths*.

Intermediate state "Bardo" in Tibetan. The state between death and rebirth. It begins the moment the consciousness leaves the body, and ceases the moment the consciousness enters the body of the next life. See *Joyful Path of Good Fortune*.

Je Tsongkhapa (AD 1357-1419) An emanation of the Wisdom Buddha Manjushri, whose appearance in fourteenth-century Tibet as a monk, and the holder of the lineage of pure view and pure deeds, was prophesied by Buddha. He spread a very pure Buddhadharma throughout Tibet, showing how to combine the practices of Sutra and Tantra, and how to practice pure Dharma during degenerate times. His tradition later became known as the "Gelug," or "Ganden Tradition." See *Heart Jewel* and *Great Treasury of Merit*.

Kadampa Tradition The pure tradition of Buddhism established by Atisha. Followers of this tradition up to the time of Je Tsongkhapa are known as "Old Kadampas," and those after the time of Je Tsongkhapa are known as "New Kadampas." See also **New Kadampa Tradition**. See *Modern Buddhism*.

Karma A Sanskrit word meaning "action." Through the force of intention, we perform actions with our body, speech and mind, and all of these actions produce effects. The effect of virtuous actions is happiness and the effect of negative actions is suffering. See *Modern Buddhism* and *Joyful Path of Good Fortune*.

Lamrim A Tibetan term, literally meaning "stages of the path." A special arrangement of all Buddha's teachings that is easy to understand and put into practice. It reveals all the stages of the path to enlightenment. For a full commentary, see *Joyful Path of Good Fortune* and *The New Meditation Handbook*.

Living being Any being who possesses a mind that is contaminated by delusions or their imprints. Both "living being" and "sentient being" are terms used to distinguish beings whose minds are contaminated by either of these two obstructions, from Buddhas, whose minds are completely free from these obstructions.

Love A mind wishing others to be happy. There are three types: affectionate love, cherishing love and wishing love. See *Modern Buddhism, Transform Your Life* and *Joyful Path of Good Fortune*.

Lower realms The hell realm, hungry ghost realm and animal realm. See also **Samsara.**

Mahayana A Sanskrit term for "Great Vehicle," the spiritual path to great enlightenment. The Mahayana goal is to attain Buddhahood for the benefit of all living beings by completely abandoning delusions and their imprints. See *Joyful Path of Good Fortune* and *Meaningful to Behold*.

Mandala offering An offering of the entire universe visualized as a Pure Land, with all its inhabitants as pure beings. See *The New Guide to Dakini Land*.

Manjushri The embodiment of the wisdom of all the Buddhas.

Mantra A Sanskrit word, literally meaning "mind protection." Mantra protects the mind from ordinary appearances and conceptions. There are four types of mantra: mantras that are mind, mantras that are inner wind, mantras that are sound and mantras that are form. In general, there are three types of mantra recitation: verbal recitation, mental recitation and vajra recitation. See *Tantric Grounds and Paths*.

Mara "Mara" is Sanskrit for "demon," and refers to anything that obstructs the attainment of liberation or enlightenment. There are four principal types of mara: the mara of the delusions, the mara of contaminated aggregates, the mara of uncontrolled death and the Devaputra maras. Of these, only the last are actual living beings. See *The New Heart of Wisdom*.

Merit The good fortune created by virtuous actions. It is the potential power to increase our good qualities and produce happiness.

Mindfulness A mental factor that functions not to forget the object realized by the primary mind. See *How to Understand the Mind* and *Meaningful to Behold*.

New Kadampa Tradition (NKT) The union of Kadampa Buddhist Centers, an international association of study and meditation centers that follow the pure tradition of Mahayana Buddhism derived from the Buddhist meditator and scholar Je Tsongkhapa, introduced into the West by the Buddhist teacher Venerable Geshe Kelsang Gyatso Rinpoche.

Precious human life A life that has eight special freedoms and ten special endowments that make it an ideal opportunity for training the mind in all the stages of the path to enlightenment. See *Modern Buddhism*, *The New Meditation Handbook*, *The New Heart of Wisdom* and *Joyful Path of Good Fortune*.

Pride A deluded mental factor that, through considering and exaggerating one's own good qualities or possessions, feels arrogant. See *How to Understand the Mind*.

Prostration An action of showing respect with body, speech or mind. See *Joyful Path of Good Fortune* and *The Bodhisattva Vow*.

Puja A ceremony in which offerings and other acts of devotion are performed in front of holy beings.

Purification Generally, any practice that leads to the attainment of a pure body, speech or mind. More specifically, a practice for purifying negative karma by means of the four opponent powers. See *Meaningful to Behold* and *The Bodhisattva Vow*.

Realization A stable and non-mistaken experience of a virtuous object that directly protects us from suffering.

Refuge Actual protection. To go for refuge to Buddha, Dharma and Sangha means to have faith in these Three Jewels and to rely on them for protection from all fears and suffering. See *Modern Buddhism* and *Joyful Path of Good Fortune*.

Samsara This can be understood in two ways—as uninterrupted rebirth without freedom or control, or as the aggregates of a being who has taken such a rebirth. Samsara is characterized by suffering and dissatisfaction. There are six realms of samsara. Listed in ascending order according to the type of karma that causes rebirth in them, they are the realms of the hell beings, hungry ghosts, animals, human beings, demi-gods and gods. The first three are lower realms or unhappy migrations, and the second three are higher realms or happy migrations. See *Joyful Path of Good Fortune* and *The New Heart of Wisdom*.

Self-cherishing A mental attitude that considers oneself to be supremely important and precious. It is regarded as a principal object to be abandoned by Bodhisattvas. See *Modern Buddhism* and *Eight Steps to Happiness*.

Shantideva (AD 687–763) A great Indian Buddhist scholar and meditation master. He composed *Guide to the Bodhisattva's Way of Life*. See *Meaningful to Behold*.

Spiritual Guide "Guru" in Sanskrit, and "Lama" in Tibetan. A Teacher who guides us along the spiritual path. See *Modern Buddhism*, *Joyful Path of Good Fortune* and *Great Treasury of Merit*.

Stages of the path See also "**Lamrim.**"

Sutra The teachings of Buddha that are open to everyone to practice without the need for an empowerment. These include Buddha's teachings of the three turnings of the Wheel of Dharma. See *Modern Buddhism*.

Tantra Tantric teachings are distinguished from Sutra teachings in that they reveal methods for training the mind by bringing the future result, or Buddhahood, into the present path. Tantric practitioners overcome ordinary appearances and conceptions by visualizing their body, environment, enjoyments and deeds as those of a Buddha. Tantra is the supreme path to full enlightenment. Tantric practices are to be done in private and only by those who have received a Tantric empowerment. Synonymous with "Secret Mantra." See *Modern Buddhism*, *Mahamudra Tantra*, *Clear Light of Bliss* and *Tantric Grounds and Paths*.

Tathagata The Sanskrit word for "A Being Gone Beyond," which is another term for Buddha.

Three Jewels The three objects of refuge: Buddha Jewel, Dharma Jewel and Sangha Jewel. They are called "Jewels" because they are both rare and precious. See *Joyful Path of Good Fortune*.

True existence Existence in any way independent of conceptual imputation. See also **Inherent existence.**

Ultimate truth The ultimate nature of all phenomena, emptiness. See *Modern Buddhism, The New Heart of Wisdom* and *Ocean Nectar.*

Wrong awareness A cognizer that is mistaken with respect to its engaged object.

Wrong view An intellectually-formed wrong awareness that denies the existence of an object that it is necessary to understand to attain liberation or enlightenment—for example, denying the existence of enlightened beings, karma or rebirth. See *Joyful Path of Good Fortune.*

Yogi/Yogini Sanskrit words usually referring to a male or a female meditator who has attained the union of tranquil abiding and superior seeing.

Bibliography

Venerable Geshe Kelsang Gyatso Rinpoche is a highly respected meditation master and scholar of the Mahayana Buddhist tradition founded by Je Tsongkhapa. Since arriving in the West in 1977, Venerable Geshe Kelsang has worked tirelessly to establish pure Buddhadharma throughout the world. Over this period he has given extensive teachings on the major scriptures of the Mahayana. These teachings provide a comprehensive presentation of the essential Sutra and Tantra practices of Mayahana Buddhism.

BOOKS

The following books by Venerable Geshe Kelsang Gyatso Rinpoche are all published by Tharpa Publications.

The Bodhisattva Vow. A practical guide to helping others. (2nd ed., 1995)

Clear Light of Bliss. A Tantric meditation manual. (3rd ed., 2014)

Eight Steps to Happiness. The Buddhist way of loving kindness. (2nd American ed., 2012)

Essence of Vajrayana. The Highest Yoga Tantra practice of Heruka body mandala. (1997)

Great Treasury of Merit. How to rely upon a Spiritual Guide.
(2nd ed., 2015)

Guide to the Bodhisattva's Way of Life. Becoming a friend of
the world. (A translation of Shantideva's famous verse
masterpiece.) (2002)

Heart Jewel. The essential practices of Kadampa Buddhism.
(2nd ed., 1997)

How to Solve Our Human Problems. The four noble truths. (1st
American ed., 2007)

How to Understand the Mind. The nature and power of the
mind. (4th ed., 2014)

Introduction to Buddhism. An explanation of the Buddhist way
of life. (1st American ed., 2008)

Joyful Path of Good Fortune. The complete Buddhist path to
enlightenment. (2nd ed., 1995)

Living Meaningfully, Dying Joyfully. The profound practice of
transference of consciousness. (1999)

Mahamudra Tantra. The supreme Heart Jewel nectar. (2005)

Meaningful to Behold. Becoming a friend of the world.
(5th ed., 2007)

Modern Buddhism. The path of compassion and wisdom. (2nd
American ed., 2015)

The New Guide to Dakini Land. The Highest Yoga Tantra
practice of Buddha Vajrayogini. (3rd ed., 2012)

The New Heart of Wisdom. Profound teachings from Buddha's
heart (An explanation of the *Heart Sutra*) (5th ed., 2012)

The New Meditation Handbook. Meditations to make our life
happy and meaningful. (2nd American ed., 2013)

Ocean of Nectar. The true nature of all things. (1995)

The Oral Instructions of Mahamudra. The very essence of
Buddha's teachings of sutra and tantra. (2016)

Tantric Grounds and Paths. How to enter, progress on, and
   complete the Vajrayana path. (1994)
Transform Your Life. A blissful journey. (2nd American ed., 2015)
Universal Compassion. Inspiring solutions for difficult times.
   (4th ed., 2002)

SADHANAS AND OTHER BOOKLETS

Venerable Geshe Kelsang Gyatso Rinpoche has also supervised
the translation of a collection of essential sadhanas, or ritual
prayers for spiritual attainments, available in booklet or audio
formats.

Avalokiteshvara Sadhana. Prayers and requests to the Buddha
   of Compassion.
The Blissful Path. The condensed self-generation sadhana of
   Vajrayogini.
The Bodhisattva's Confession of Moral Downfalls. The purification
   practice of the *Mahayana Sutra of the Three Superior Heaps*.
Condensed Essence of Vajrayana. Condensed Heruka body
   mandala self-generation sadhana.
Dakini Yoga. The middling self-generation sadhana of
   Vajrayogini.
Drop of Essential Nectar. A special fasting and purification
   practice in conjunction with Eleven-faced Avalokiteshvara.
Essence of Good Fortune. Prayers for the six preparatory
   practices for meditation on the stages of the path to
   enlightenment.
Essence of Vajrayana. Heruka body mandala self-generation
   sadhana according to the system of Mahasiddha Ghantapa.
Feast of Great Bliss. Vajrayogini self-initiation sadhana.

Great Liberation of the Father. Preliminary prayers for Mahamudra meditation in conjunction with Heruka practice.

Great Liberation of the Mother. Preliminary prayers for Mahamudra meditation in conjunction with Vajrayogini practice.

The Great Mother. A method to overcome hindrances and obstacles by reciting the *Essence of Wisdom Sutra* (the *Heart Sutra*).

A Handbook for the Daily Practice of Bodhisattva Vows and Tantric Vows.

Heartfelt Prayers. Funeral service for cremations and burials.

Heart Jewel. The Guru yoga of Je Tsongkhapa combined with the condensed sadhana of his Dharma Protector.

The Kadampa Way of Life. The essential practice of Kadam Lamrim.

Keajra Heaven. The essential commentary to the practice of *The Uncommon Yoga of Inconceivability.*

Liberation from Sorrow. Praises and requests to the Twenty-one Taras.

Mahayana Refuge Ceremony and Bodhisattva Vow Ceremony.

Medicine Buddha Prayer. A method for benefiting others.

Medicine Buddha Sadhana. A method for accomplishing the attainments of Medicine Buddha.

Meditation and Recitation of Solitary Vajrasattva.

Melodious Drum Victorious in all Directions. The extensive fulfilling and restoring ritual of the Dharma Protector, the great king Dorje Shugden, in conjunction with Mahakala, Kalarupa, Kalindewi and other Dharma Protectors.

Offering to the Spiritual Guide (Lama Chopa). A special way of relying upon a Spiritual Guide.

Path of Compassion for the Deceased. Powa sadhana for the benefit of the deceased

Pathway to the Pure Land. Training in powa—the transference of consciousness.

Powa Ceremony. Transference of consciousness for the deceased.

Prayers for Meditation. Brief preparatory prayers for meditation.

Prayers for World Peace.

A Pure Life. The practice of taking and keeping the eight Mahayana precepts.

Quick Path to Great Bliss. The extensive self-generation sadhana of Vajrayogini.

The Root Tantra of Heruka and Vajrayogini. Chapters One and Fifty-one of the *Condensed Heruka Root Tantra.*

The Root Text: Eight Verses of Training the Mind.

Treasury of Wisdom. The sadhana of Venerable Manjushri.

The Uncommon Yoga of Inconceivability The special instruction of how to reach the Pure Land of Keajra with this human body.

Union of No More Learning. Heruka body mandala self-initiation sadhana.

Vajra Hero Yoga. The brief practice of Heruka body mandala self-generation.

The Vows and Commitments of Kadampa Buddhism.

Wishfulfilling Jewel. The Guru yoga of Je Tsongkhapa combined with the sadhana of his Dharma Protector.

The Yoga of Buddha Amitayus. A special method for increasing lifespan, wisdom and merit.

The Yoga of Buddha Heruka. The essential self-generation sadhana of Heruka body mandala & Condensed six-session yoga.

The Yoga of Buddha Maitreya. Self-generation sadhana.

The Yoga of Buddha Vajrapani. Self-generation sadhana.

The Yoga of Enlightened Mother Arya Tara. Self-generation sadhana.

The Yoga of Great Mother Prajnaparamita. Self-generation sadhana.

The Yoga of Thousand-armed Avalokiteshvara. Self-generation sadhana.

The Yoga of White Tara, Buddha of Long Life.

To order any of our products please visit www.tharpa.com or contact your nearest Tharpa office (see page 165).

NKT – IKBU

Study Programs of Kadampa Buddhism

Kadampa Buddhism is a Mahayana Buddhist school founded by the great Indian Buddhist Master Atisha (AD 982–1054). His followers are known as "Kadampas." "Ka" means "word" and refers to Buddha's teachings, and "dam" refers to Atisha's special Lamrim instructions known as "the stages of the path to enlightenment." By integrating their knowledge of all Buddha's teachings into their practice of Lamrim, and by integrating this into their everyday lives, Kadampa Buddhists are encouraged to use Buddha's teachings as practical methods for transforming daily activities into the path to enlightenment. The great Kadampa Teachers are famous not only for being great scholars, but also for being spiritual practitioners of immense purity and sincerity.

The lineage of these teachings, both their oral transmission and blessings, was then passed from Teacher to disciple, spreading throughout much of Asia, and now to many countries throughout the Western world. Buddha's teachings, which are known as "Dharma," are likened to a wheel that moves from country to country in accordance with changing conditions and people's karmic inclinations. The external forms of presenting Buddhism may change as it meets with different cultures and societies, but its essential authenticity is ensured through the continuation of an unbroken lineage of realized practitioners.

Kadampa Buddhism was first introduced into the West in 1977 by the renowned Buddhist Master, Venerable Geshe Kelsang Gyatso Rinpoche. Since that time he has worked tirelessly to spread Kadampa Buddhism throughout the world by giving extensive teachings, writing many profound texts on Kadampa Buddhism and founding the New Kadampa Tradition–International Kadampa Buddhist Union (NKT-IKBU), which now has over a thousand Kadampa Buddhist Centers and groups worldwide. Each Center offers study programs on Buddhist psychology, philosophy and meditation instruction, as well as retreats for all levels of practitioner. The emphasis is on integrating Buddha's teachings into daily life to solve our human problems and to spread lasting peace and happiness throughout the world.

The Kadampa Buddhism of the NKT-IKBU is an entirely independent Buddhist tradition and has no political affiliations. It is an association of Buddhist Centers and practitioners that derive their inspiration and guidance from the example of the ancient Kadampa Buddhist Masters and their teachings, as presented by Venerable Geshe Kelsang.

There are three reasons why we need to study and practice the teachings of Buddha: to develop our wisdom, to cultivate a good heart and to maintain a peaceful state of mind. If we do not strive to develop our wisdom, we will always remain ignorant of ultimate truth—the true nature of reality. Although we wish for happiness, our ignorance leads us to engage in non-virtuous actions, which are the main cause of all our suffering. If we do not cultivate a good heart, our selfish motivation destroys harmony and good relationships with others. We have no peace, and no chance to gain pure happiness. Without inner peace, outer peace is impossible. If we do not maintain a peaceful state of mind, we are not happy even if we have ideal conditions. On the other hand, when our mind is peaceful, we are happy, even if our external conditions are unpleasant. Therefore, the development of these qualities is of utmost importance for our daily happiness.

Venerable Geshe Kelsang Gyatso, or "Geshe-la" as he is affectionately called by his students, has designed three special spiritual programs for the systematic study and practice of Kadampa Buddhism that are especially suited to the modern world—the General Program (GP), the Foundation Program (FP) and the Teacher Training Program (TTP).

GENERAL PROGRAM

The General Program provides a basic introduction to Buddhist view, meditation and practice that is suitable for beginners. It also includes advanced teachings and practice from both Sutra and Tantra.

FOUNDATION PROGRAM

The Foundation Program provides an opportunity to deepen our understanding and experience of Buddhism through a systematic study of six texts:

1. *Joyful Path of Good Fortune*—a commentary to Atisha's Lamrim instructions, the stages of the path to enlightenment.
2. *Universal Compassion*—a commentary to Bodhisattva Chekhawa's *Training the Mind in Seven Points*.

3. *Eight Steps to Happiness*—a commentary to Bodhisattva Langri Tangpa's *Eight Verses of Training the Mind.*

4. *The New Heart of Wisdom*—a commentary to the *Heart Sutra.*

5. *Meaningful to Behold*—a commentary to Bodhisattva Shantideva's *Guide to the Bodhisattva's Way of Life.*

6. *How to Understand the Mind*—a detailed explanation of the mind, based on the works of the Buddhist scholars Dharmakirti and Dignaga.

The benefits of studying and practicing these texts are as follows:

(1) *Joyful Path of Good Fortune*—we gain the ability to put all Buddha's teachings of both Sutra and Tantra into practice. We can easily make progress on and complete, the stages of the path to the supreme happiness of enlightenment. From a practical point of view, Lamrim is the main body of Buddha's teachings, and the other teachings are like its limbs.

(2) and (3) *Universal Compassion* and *Eight Steps to Happiness*— we gain the ability to integrate Buddha's teachings into our daily life and solve all our human problems.

(4) *The New Heart of Wisdom*—we gain a realization of the ultimate nature of reality. By gaining this realization, we can eliminate the ignorance of self-grasping, which is the root of all our suffering.

(5) *Meaningful to Behold*—we transform our daily activities into the Bodhisattva's way of life, thereby making every moment of our human life meaningful.

(6) *How to Understand the Mind*—we understand the relationship between our mind and its external objects. If we understand

that objects depend on the subjective mind, we can change the way objects appear to us by changing our own mind. Gradually we will gain the ability to control our mind and in this way, solve all our problems.

TEACHER TRAINING PROGRAM

The Teacher Training Program is designed for people who wish to train as authentic Dharma Teachers. In addition to completing the study of fourteen texts of Sutra and Tantra, which include the six texts mentioned above, students are required to observe certain commitments with regard to behavior and way of life, and to complete a number of meditation retreats.

A Special Teacher Training Program is also held at KMC London, England, and can be studied at the Center or by correspondence. This special meditation and study program consists of six courses spread over three years based on the books of Venerable Geshe Kelsang: *How to Understand the Mind, Modern Buddhism, The New Heart of Wisdom, Tantric Grounds and Paths,* Shantideva's *Guide to the Bodhisattva's Way of Life* and its commentary, *Meaningful to Behold* and *Ocean of Nectar.*

All Kadampa Buddhist Centers are open to the public. Every year we celebrate Festivals in many countries throughout the world, including two in England, where people gather from around the world to receive special teachings and empowerments and to enjoy a spiritual vacation. Please feel free to visit us any time!

For further information about NKT-IKBU study programs
or to find your nearest center, visit
www.kadampa.org or contact:

US NKT-IKBU Office
Kadampa Meditation Center New York
47 Sweeney Road
Glen Spey, NY 12737
USA

Phone: 845-856-9000
Toll free: 877-523-2672
Fax: 845-856-2110

E-mail: info@kadampanewyork.org
Website: www.kadampanewyork.org

NKT-IKBU Central Office
Conishead Priory
Ulverston
Cumbria, LA12 9QQ
England

Phone: 01229-588533
Fax: 01229-580080

E-mail: info@kadampa.org
Website: www.kadampa.org

Tharpa Publications Worldwide

*B*ooks from Tharpa Publications are currently published in English (American and British), Chinese, French, German, Italian, Japanese, Portuguese and Spanish. Most languages are available from any Tharpa Publications office listed below.

Visit us at www.Tharpa.com or contact your
local office for more information.

United States

Tharpa Publications US
47 Sweeney Road
Glen Spey, NY 12737
Phone: 845-856-5102
Fax: 845-856-2110
E-mail: info.us@tharpa.com
www.tharpa.com/us

Asia

Tharpa Asia
1/F, Causeway Tower,
16-22 Causeway Road,
Causeway Bay, Hong Kong
Tel: (852) 2507 2237
Fax: (852) 2507 2208
Email: info.asia@tharpa.com
www.tharpa.com/hk-en

Brazil

Editoria Tharpa Brasil
Rua Fradique Coutinho, 701
Pinheiros, 05416-011
São Paulo - SP
Phone: +55 (11) 3476-2328
E-mail: contato.br@tharpa.com
www.tharpa.com/br

United Kingdom

Tharpa Publications UK
Conishead Priory
Ulverston, Cumbria,
LA12 9QQ
Phone: +44 (0)1229-588599
E-mail: info.uk@tharpa.com
www.tharpa.com/uk

Australia

Tharpa Publications Australia
25 McCarthy Road
Monbulk VIC 3793
Phone: +61 (0)3 9752 0377
E-mail: info.au@tharpa.com
www.tharpa.com/au

Canada

Tharpa Publications Canada
631 Crawford St.
Toronto, ON, M6G 3K1
Phone: 416-762-8710
Fax: 416-762-2267
E-mail: info.ca@tharpa.com
www.tharpa.com/ca

France

Editions Tharpa
Château de Segrais
72220 Saint-Mars-d'Outillé
Phone: +33 (0)2 43 87 71 02
E-mail: info.fr@tharpa.com
www.tharpa.com/fr

Japan

Tharpa Japan
166-0004 Tokyo-bu
Suginami-ku, Minami
Asagaya 2-21-19
Phone/Fax: + 81(0)03-3312-0021
E-mail: info@kadampa.jp
www.tharpa.com/jp

Portugal

Publicações Tharpa Portugal
Rua Moinho do Gato, 5
Várzea de Sintra
2710-661 Sintra
Phone: +351 219231064
E-mail: info.pt@tharpa.com
www.tharpa.pt

Spain

Editorial Tharpa España
Calle Manuela Malasaña No
26
28004 Madrid
Phone: +34 91 7557535
E-mail: info.es@tharpa.com
www.tharpa.com/es

Germany

Tharpa-Verlag Deutschland
Mehringdamm 33, Aufgang 2
10961 Berlin
Phone: +49 (030) 430 55 666
E-mail: info.de@tharpa.com
www.tharpa.com/de

Mexico

Tharpa Mexico
Enrique Rébsamen No. 406
Col. Narvate Poniente
C.P. 03020, México, D.F.
Phone: +52 56 39 61 86
Phone/Fax: +52 56 39 61 80
E-mail: info.mx@tharpa.com
www.tharpa.com/mx

Republic of South Africa

c/o Mahasiddha KMC
24 Shongweni Heights
5 Angus Drive, Hillcrest
Durban, 3610
Phone: +27 (0)31 464 0984
Fax: +27(0)86-513-34-76
E-mail: info.za@tharpa.com
www.tharpa.com/za

Switzerland

Tharpa Verlag Schwiez
Mirabellenstrasse 1
CH-8048 Zürich
Phone: +41 44 401 02 20
E-mail: info.ch@tharpa.com
www.tharpa.com/ch

Index

The letter "g" indicates an entry in the glossary

Breathing Med. to accomplish 4 things:

Suggested Reading

If you enjoyed *How to Solve Our Human Problems*, the following books will help deepen your understanding and practical experience of the path to liberation and enlightenment. As the author says in *Modern Buddhism,* "If everyone sincerely practices the path of compassion and wisdom, all their problems will be solved and never arise again; I guarantee this."

Venerable Geshe Kelsang Gyatso Rinpoche, an internationally renowned teacher and meditation master, is the author of a completely integrated collection of authentic Buddhist teachings acclaimed for their clarity and practical application.

Transform Your Life
A Blissful Journey

A perfect manual for inner transformation, this book reveals how we can discover the real meaning of our human life and fulfill our human potential to find everlasting peace and happiness.

Paperback · $16.95 · 400 pp   ePub/Kindle $9.99
Audiobook · $34.95 · 8 CDs/9 hrs MP3 $18.99

Modern Buddhism
The Path of Compassion and Wisdom

A special presentation of Buddha's teachings on developing and maintaining compassion and wisdom in daily life to solve all our daily problems.

Paperback · $16.95 · 464 pp
Audiobook · $34.95 · 8 CDs/9 hrs MP3 $18.99
Free eBook and pdf at: www.emodernbuddhism.com

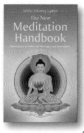

The New Meditation Handbook
Meditations to Make our Life Happy and Meaningful

Clear instructions on 21 step-by-step Lamrim meditations that together comprise the entire Buddhist path to temporary and ultimate happiness, or enlightenment.

Paperback · $14.95 · 240 pp   ePub/Kindle $8.99
Audiobook · $19.95 · 4 CDs/5 hrs MP3 $14.99

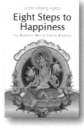

Eight Steps to Happiness
The Buddhist Way of Loving Kindness

Based on the poem *Eight Verses for Training the Mind*, this book reveals the practice of taking and giving to help transform adverse conditions into spiritual insights.

Paperback · $16.95 · 384 pp   ePub/Kindle $9.99
Audiobook · $34.95 · 7 CDs/8 hrs MP3 $18.99

Available from your favorite bookstore or online at www.tharpa.com/us

Suggested Listening

Improve your daily practice using these CDs
breathing and visualization meditations guided by an experienced meditator

Meditations for Relaxation
three guided meditations to relax body and mind

Meditations for a Clear Mind
finding happiness from a different source

Meditations for a Kind Heart
the healing power of cherishing others

$12.95 each (includes a 16 page booklet)

"Our meditation should not be like the flight of a small bird, which never stops flapping its wings and is always changing direction, but like the flight of an eagle, which soars gently with only occasional adjustments to its wings."
~Geshe Kelsang Gyatso in *Modern Buddhism* (page 138-39)

Helpful Resources

VISIT OUR WEBSITE www.tharpa.com/us
  ◆ See our complete line of books, eBooks, audio, artwork and meditation supplies.
  ◆ Sign up for our newsletter to be notified of new products and special offers (we never share our Email list)

FIND A MEDITATION CLASS www.map.kadampa.org
  ◆ There are over 250 Kadampa meditation centers and groups across the US
  ◆ Contact the center near you for a schedule of events

LEARN ABOUT THE TEMPLES PROJECT www.kadampatemples.org
  ◆ Tharpa profits are donated to the International Temples Project
  ◆ Your purchases help build Kadampa World Peace Temples (see back cover flap)

FOLLOW US ON SOCIAL MEDIA Facebook & Twitter

 facebook.com/
TharpaUs

 twitter.com/
TharpaUs

CONTACT THARPA PUBLICATIONS for more details, meditation classes near you or any other information:
47 Sweeney Rd, Glen Spey, NY 12737 ◆ info.us@tharpa.com ◆ (845) 856-5102 or toll free (888) 741-3475

Available from your favorite bookstore or online at www.tharpa.com/us